Developing the Complete You

Spirit . . . Soul . . . Body

REGINALD EZELL

Order this book online at www.trafford.com
or email orders@trafford.com

Most Trafford titles are also available at major online book retailers.

Print information available on the last page.

ISBN: 978-1-4907-7821-1 (sc)
ISBN: 978-1-4907-7820-4 (hc)
ISBN: 978-1-4907-7822-8 (e)

Library of Congress Control Number: 2016917852

KJV
Scripture quotations marked KJV are from the Holy Bible, King James Version
(Authorized Version). First published in 1611. Quoted from the KJV Classic
Reference Bible, Copyright © 1983 by The Zondervan Corporation.

Trafford rev.   10/29/2016

 www.trafford.com

North America & international
toll-free: 1 888 232 4444 (USA & Canada)
fax: 812 355 4082

DEDICATION

I dedicate this book, Developing the Complete You
Spirit . . . Soul . . . Body, to my wife, Wanta' Ezell.

I thank you for being such a powerful force with
me as we win souls for the Kingdom of God. I look
forward to seeing along with you the lives of men and
women developed into the fullness of who God called
them to be. Thank you for all your love, prayers, and
support. You truly are a good thing from the Lord.

I love you, Wanta'.

CONTENTS

CHAPTER 1

The Father—Developing the Spirit

A Relationship with the Father Develops Our Spirit

The primary responsibility of a pastor is to assist God in developing, growing, and maturing believers into the vessels that God wants them to be. In conjunction with that, God's people must be willing to be pliable, not to the pastor, but to God. Every child of God has to be ready to hear God's voice, understand what He is saying, and be willing to change as He directs. Change is a good thing, and it is necessary. You cannot stay the same or have the same mentality and perform a different action from your current thought process. Please understand that if your desire is to do something different, you have to become something different. Doing the same things and expecting different results is insanity, and that is why change is necessary.

Salvation is the constant process of change, and it is God's plan for us to be changed from the way we used to think. Unfortunately, as members of the body of Christ, we have not fully comprehended the whole master plan of God. Many have understood and grasped certain areas, but for the most part, we are not totally focused on what God is trying to do in our lives. We do not always comprehend as we should, so there is a need for us to learn and recognize God's plan of salvation for us.

Developing the Complete You was written for this very reason. Through this study, it is my prayer that God will help us understand how we get to the place that is necessary for us to fulfill God's will. Most people do understand that God is their source; however, there is an ultimate place that God wants us to be. *Developing the Complete You* is an attempt to get every believer who allows these words into their hearts to change them for the better, forever! So let us begin with how our relationship with our heavenly Father develops our spirit.

Created in His Image

1 Thessalonians 5:23–24 says, for us to *be preserved blameless unto the coming of our Lord Jesus Christ. Faithful is he that calleth you, who also will do it.* According to these verses, we are supposed to be a certain way when Jesus comes, and God is able to help us reach that destination. Many Christians want to know and operate in God's perfect will; but when we do not understand how God develops us, His desires become difficult to accomplish. We need to learn who God is and how He does what He does in us.

God is a triune God, just as man is a triune being. God is also the God of divine order as well as divine purpose, and He does nothing by accident. God has also preordained and pre-established our lives. When God did what He did during creation, He had an exact picture in His mind of what He was doing, but it is not like that with many of us. We want to check if certain things are going to work before we take action. Unlike us, God already knows how things are going to work. We want to see if certain things are going to work. God already knows what is supposed to happen, and we can see this as He demonstrates the surety of His plan in the book of Genesis.

The story of the creation of mankind may be elementary to some, but I want you to get a full understanding of *how* man was created. For many, this will be a new level of ministry and a new level of the church, as you have understood. To get a better understanding of this, we will have to put away old ways, old thoughts, and old habits. It is vitally important that we start looking at the *specifics* of God's words and not just the generality of His words.

Many people have kept God in a general place in their lives and not in a specific place. Thus, we are not maximizing the full potential of who God is at the same time not maximizing the full potential of the Trinity of God. I thank God for Jesus. I thank God for the Holy Spirit. I thank God in everything. However, we will never understand the fullness of the benefits of Jesus or of the Holy Spirit until we know all the benefits of God the Father.

Genesis 1:26 says, *And God, said let us make man in our image.* Notice, He said "our" image. God is talking in the sense of "me, mine, and ours." In this verse, God has already acknowledged the Trinity of Himself. He said "let us" because the Trinity is real to Him. God the Father, God the Son, and God the Holy Spirit are the "us" that made man in their image and after "their" likeness. It is not a coincidence that God is a triune being and that He made man a triune being. If God is going to make man in His own image and likeness, He had to make man like Himself. Understand that God is three persons in one, and all three make up the Godhead. This is just how we are: three entities in one (spirit, soul, and body), and this makes us like God.

Unfortunately, we sometimes generalize our creation. In the Old Testament, God was still unified in himself. There was not much clarity of the differences of God. The translators interchanged the words *Lord* and *God*; however, they were talking about all three. It did not matter whether one part was doing the work or not, they were still God. All three were three in one.

In the New Testament, we begin to see the distinction, separation, functions, and benefits of the three parts of God. Yet we still generalize it and put them in one. We still keep them grouped together even though they are separate in their workings, trying to bring the unity and oneness back. I remember teaching a message on the final level where I outlined how the Father, the Son, and the Holy Spirit wanted to reunite again in you. The final level is when you connect all three of Him as one in you. It is when all of you and all of Him become one together.

Different Parts Develop Different Functions

Each part of God develops a different part of man. Each part of God must be targeted toward the right part of man, or you will never get all the benefits or the fullness of any part. The order is very specific. It is just like eating. If I eat physical food, it is going to benefit my physical body. However, eating the physical food will not benefit my spirit until I start eating spiritual food (the word of God). In other words, my physical body will be benefiting and receiving from the physical food, but not all three parts of me. My mind does not fully grow by physical food alone. I do realize some foods are called "brain" foods, but I do not know if that makes you smart or not. Nevertheless, the primary benefit of food is specifically for the body, more than anything else.

The primary part of man that God wants to develop and establish is our spirit man, which is the main part of us. The Holy Spirit does not develop the primary part of our spirit man; however, the Holy Spirit can help. Neither is our spirit man primarily developed by Jesus the word, even though Jesus can help. Our spirit man is developed primarily by our intimate, personal one-on-one relationship with the Father. There is no getting around the fact that there is no substitute for your personal relationship with God. This is something that nobody can do for you, stand in proxy for you, intercede on your behalf, or be an alternate for you. It is between you and God alone.

Being Whole

The entirety of 1 Thessalonians 5:23 says, *And the very God of peace sanctify you wholly; and I pray God your whole spirit and soul and body be preserved blameless unto the coming of our Lord Jesus Christ.* Peace in this verse means shalom, and peace means more than just calmness. The Hebrew word for peace (shalom) means nothing missing, nothing broken, and nothing lacking. This peace signifies that God is fullness and He is the very God of wholeness.

Our heavenly Father is the very God of peace, who will sanctify you, set you apart, separate, isolate, and cover you. Think of it as being similar to a caterpillar inside a chrysalis before it transforms into a butterfly, or like a yolk in an egg before it becomes a baby chick. Shalom (God's peace) is that protection; it is that covering, that wholeness. When a caterpillar is inside a chrysalis, it does not have to worry about anything because everything it needs is there inside the covering. The yolk in the egg does not have to worry about air, food, or anything else for that matter. Everything the yolk needs is self-contained inside the egg's shell.

Likewise, everything we need today is self-contained in God. We must understand who God is and accept His words and His wisdom. God wants to be the very God of peace who will sanctify us completely. He wants to sanctify wholly our spirit, soul, and body because man is a triune being. Man is a spirit who possesses a soul and lives in a body. The fullness of man is wholeness in spirit, soul, and body.

You are not all spirit, all soul, or all body, but the three together complete you. You can have a body lying on a bed, but if it does not have a soul or mind with brain waves, you are considered brain-dead. So it is the fullness of who you are that God wants to mature, thereby making your life complete.

The True Worshiper

The books of the Gospel – (Matthew, Mark, Luke, and John) is primarily the same account of the life of Jesus, with some differences in views and perceptions. Yet John had a revelation that the others did not have. He perceived the Father's love. John wrote,

> *Jesus saith unto her, Woman, believe me, the hour cometh, when ye shall neither in this mountain, nor yet at Jerusalem, worship the Father. Ye worship ye know not what: we know what we worship: for salvation is of the Jews. But the hour cometh, and now is, when the true worshippers shall worship the Father in spirit and in truth: for the Father seeketh such to worship him.* (John 4:21–23)

Jesus mentioned the word "now," but when is now and why did He mention it? Now always starts immediately. It is not yesterday, and it is not going to be tomorrow. Your now is now. *The hour has come and "now is"*, was a statement of great importance then and is still significant today. *Now is the hour* and right after this statement Jesus ties it in with *the true worshippers*. This is an indication that there were other worshippers, but they were not true worshippers.

Many people have been worshipping God, but the true worshippers are going to worship the Father. The true worshippers shall worship the Father in spirit and in truth. So, the developing of your spirit is based upon your relationship and *worship* with the Father.

This fact brings us to the importance of prayer. This time of worship is precious, and when it comes down to spending time with God in prayer, please do not waste your time praying with problems on your mind. Also, do not waste your time in prayer concerning yourself with the devil. You will never benefit from all that God has, unless you are spending intimate time with Him free of distractions.

Let's compare this to spending quiet time with your spouse. You may have kids around you all of the time, or you may be facing various types of personal issues, but eventually you will finally get some quiet time with your spouse. Unfortunately, many people choose to spend that quiet time talking about problems instead of taking advantage of it. I understand that there may be things going on that require your attention, but do not make that same mistake with God. For example, while you are on your job, you think about your job, but when you go to pray, it should be an intimate time spent with God; you should not bring your job or your problems into your prayer time. You should not even bring in the trouble that the devil is trying to inflict on you. Forget him. The devil is not the issue. The issue is the lack of your personal relationship with God the Father. When you know Him, the devil is not a problem.

Again, prayer is important and there is a proper way of praying. Jesus said not to ask Him anything, but to go to the *Father* in His name. What He wants you to do is get to know who the Father is and make sure you are secure in who you are. When you develop in this it is not going to matter what is going on around you. John 4:24 says, *God is a spirit, and they that worship must worship Him in spirit and in truth.* John 4:23 also says, *For the father seeketh such to worship Him.* Notice what the Father is seeking. Is God seeking someone who wants to complain to Him and tell Him all of their problems? No, He is seeking someone who wants to worship.

Spend Your Prayer Time Wisely

Think about this concept in an earthly sense. Suppose you have a great relationship with your natural father; when you spend time together, will you talk to him about all the things you need, or will you just simply enjoy his presence?

How do you spend time with God? Do you spend time with God only when you go to Him for the things you need, or do you simply take advantage of His presence? When you spend time with God, are you talking about all the things that have gone wrong in your life, or are you developing and cultivating a relationship with Him? Once you cultivate that relationship, you are going to realize that everything that concerns you concerns Him. His love is so great for you that there is nothing He will not do for you. There is nothing that He will restrain from you that you do not even have to ask Him for. Before you ask, He already knows you have need of these things (Matthew 6:8, 32; Luke 12:32). Still, the word will not have full effect until you develop a relationship with Him.

And when thou prayest, thou shalt not be as the hypocrites are (Matthew 6:5). Another issue for some believers is that the time in prayer is not about the relationship; it is about being seen. It is not about the cultivation. Some are doing it for show and for form. The only time they communicate with God is when they come in front of everybody else so that they can look like everybody else. That is hypocrisy.

Do not be like that. Your prayer time is just you and Him, Matthew 6:5 says,

> *For they love to pray standing in the synagogues and in the corners of the streets, that they may be seen of men. Verily I say unto you, They have their reward. But thou, when thou prayest, enter into thy closet, and when thou hast shut thy door, pray to thy Father which is in secret; and thy Father which seeth in secret shall reward thee openly.*

In the Amplified Bible, it says when you pray go into your most private room. You see, the closet is the place you do not bring your entire problem, your in-laws, your ex, your stepchildren—you do not bring any of that. Your closet is your most private room where it is just you and Him. Your problems have to be left outside, because there is no room for it. All of your relatives have to be left outside, because there is only room for you and the Father.

When you get there, everything else is going to be dealt with because when you rub on Him, He rubs on you. When you love Him, He loves you. Everything seems to just work out. When you leave, you are not the same person you were when you came in, and you do not pick up what you laid down.

Remember, God is seeking true worshippers to do so in spirit and in truth.. Allow me to illustrate how I approach the Father when I go into my closet. Before I go in, I am going to lay my problems down; I am going to empty out of me anything that will distract me from receiving in His presence. When I get in there, that empty space that was filled by that problem is going to be filled by Him. When I leave there, I do not have faith for the problem anymore. It cannot even come into my life anymore. Why? I have replaced that problem with Him. However, if you bring the problems inside the room, you will not have space for Him, so leave it outside. He is going to replace the problem with the solution. He is going to replace the lack with the provision. You cannot bring the lack in the room. What are you going to do with it when you get there? God cannot pour into a cup that is already full.

In the Old Testament, when the veil was still there, they would not go behind the veil unclean. That was why they got rid of everything before they got there. They could not take any unclean and unwanted thing in. They had to leave it outside. We do not need to come to him like that today, but we should leave everything outside and go to the Lord. In the Old Testament, they cleaned and washed their hands, and they offered burnt offerings and sacrifices before going behind the veil. (Before they went in, they tied a rope and a bell to their feet. Therefore, if the person went in unclean, they would fall out. The others would hear the bell and as long as the bells could be heard, the others would know that they were still alive and had been accepted by God. They would not go in to get the person for fear of being unclean and having the same fate.)

If you have any unclean issues with you leave that mess outside. It is not like God the Father does not know or is not concerned, He cannot give you the answer when you are focused on the problem. Unless you do not want to hear the answer. Maybe you just want to talk about the problem. I suggest if you want to be a true worshiper and develop a relationship with God, that you leave your dilemma outside. Do not get in that place, the closet, and waste your time.

Matthew 6:8 says, *Be not ye therefore like unto them: for your Father knoweth what things ye have need of, before ye ask him.* When you are in that place, after this manner, therefore pray, *"Our father . . ."* You are going to change what comes out of your mouth when you change your heart toward Him. Your issues would be how much more can I get of Him? How much closer can I get to Him? How much of me can die to see more of Him? How much of Him can come into me?

How much of His influence can be upon me? How much of His understanding can be through me? That's what I want. Is that what you want? This is not a book for new beginners. This is a book for those that want a new beginning and want to do it right. We have gone through the motions, and we have gone through all these things. Now, we want to allow the fullness of His will to manifest not just in our minds, but through our lives. We want people to see a change, to see a difference, and to experience the God in us in all that we do. It cannot happen unless we yield and have an intimate, personal one-on-one relationship with the Father to where He is the most important thing. Once that happens, everything else will line up.

God's Purpose and the Importance of Jesus

You will never understand the fullness of what Jesus did until you know why God did it. What was stolen and broken in the garden when Adam sinned? It was a relationship with the Father. What did Jesus come to restore? It was a relationship with the Father.

Yet what are you seeking? If you are not seeking the relationship with the Father, then you will never know the place and importance of Jesus in your life.

What is the main difference in religions? Most religions believe there is a God, but the difference is Jesus. Some people believe in Jesus, but the difference they have is what position Jesus holds. John 5:30 says, *I can of mine own self do nothing: as I hear, I judge:*

and my judgment is just; because I seek not mine own will, but the will of the Father which hath sent me.

We understand the concept of three in one which is the Trinity. We know Jesus, who is part of the Trinity, and we recognize and separate the importance of the Father in Jesus' life, but why are we still going to generalize God in our own lives? You will never be able to do all you do by generalizing or making God's role (Father, Son & Holy Spirit) common. Jesus did not do that. Jesus, who is part of the Trinity of God, said He could do nothing on his own. If Jesus needs a relationship with the Father, what makes you think you can do anything without that relationship with the Father?

> John 5:31,33,43 says, *If I bear witness of myself, my witness is not true. There is another that beareth witness of me; and I know that the witness which he witnesseth of me is true. Ye sent unto John, and he bare witness unto the truth. I am come in my Father's name, and ye receive me not: if another shall come in his own name, him ye will receive.*

How *did* Jesus come? Did He come in His own name, or did He come in the Father's name? What made Jesus so awesomely blessed and able to succeed in all that He did? The answer is in this statement. Jesus said, *I do nothing but what the Father tells me to do. I say nothing but what the Father tells me to say. I go no place than but where the Father sends me* (John 5:43).

What makes people think that they can do what they do without the Father? The truth is that we cannot, yet we are not cultivating that relationship with the Father like Jesus did. Most Christians are getting all the word they can handle; however, they have more word and understanding of that word than they will ever walk in.

Whatever problem you have or facing, you have the word for the answer. God will not allow the problem to come before He allows the word to come. The problem only comes because of the word that was sown in you. You see, when you are saved in God, it is not a fair fight, or even a losing fight. God is never going to allow you to face something greater than you. He is going to always put more of Him in you before He allows it to come to you. He is only allowing it to come so that He can show you who you really are.

> *I am one that bear witness of myself, and the Father that sent me beareth witness of me. Then said they unto him, Where is thy Father? Jesus answered; Ye neither know me, nor my Father: if ye had known me, ye should have known my Father also.* (John 8:18–19)

I am trying to help you understand that we can worship God, and God will receive that worship. However, we should start being mindful that God is three in one, God the Father, God the Son, and God the Holy Spirit, so we can see what part of us needs what part of Him. And we can direct our actions toward the appropriate part. If you do not identify the spirit, soul, and body part of you, how can you maximize who you are? You will have to take note of what you are and the part of you that needs development.

For example, if you have no revelation, understanding, or separation of your flesh, how would you know to exercise or eat properly? How would you know to do anything that will cultivate and make it better if you do not identify that there is a part of you that is called the "fleshy" part? Some people do not pay attention to that part until it becomes a problem. If you do not take note of your state of mind and understand that your mind needs to be renewed, then how will you ever begin to change your approach or your actions toward anything?

I want you to understand that you must identify the 3 parts of you, as well as the three parts of God. After that, you will need to target those separate parts of Him toward the separate parts of you. This is the only way you are going to maximize who He is and maximize who you are supposed to be.

Distinguishing the Roles and the Importance of Each

> *Jesus answered them, I told you, and ye believed not:*
> *the works that I do in my Father's name, they bear*
> *witness of me. But ye believe not, because ye are not of*
> *my sheep, as I said unto you. My sheep hear my voice,*
> *and I know them, and they follow me: And I give*
> *unto them eternal life; and they shall never perish,*
> *neither shall any man pluck them out of my hand.*
> *My father, which gave them me, is greater than all;*
> *and no man is able to pluck them out of my father's*
> *hand. I and my father are one.* (John 10:25–30)

Jesus and the Father are one. Jesus prayed a prayer *I pray that you are one with me, even as I and my Father are one.* Here you see the distinct difference that He acknowledges the greater one in His life. I thank God for Jesus and we should never lessen the importance of Jesus because He connects us to God.

Consequently, you will never know the importance of Jesus until you know the Father, or more importantly, until you know the Father's love. When the Bible says that *God so loved the world that He gave His only begotten son*, which part of God gave His son? It was the Father. So which part loved the world so much? It was the Father. That is why we should want the Father's love. So why not seek the Father's attention?

John 14:6 says, *Jesus saith unto him, I am the way, the truth, and the life: no man cometh unto the Father, but by me.* Jesus is the way to whom? Jesus is the truth to what? No man can come to whom and by way of whom? As you can see, Jesus is not the destination, but He is the path to the destination. If you never get to the destination, then what is the use of the path? You have your map to your destination, but you never take advantage of getting to the destination. What is the sense in having a map to get there if you do not go there?

John 14:7 says, *If ye had known me, ye should have known my Father also: and from henceforth ye know him, and have seen him.*

Jesus was saying that when people begin to know you, then they are going to see where you came from. God is not just Jesus' Father, but He is your father too. Therefore, when people know you, then they should know who your Father is. They should know because your actions, your words, your deeds, your attitudes, and your very appearance present who He is and hence who you are. When we deal with people, we make the difference, which is Jesus, the issue instead of making Jesus the way to the destination, which is to the Father.

> *Philip saith unto him, Lord, show us the Father, and it sufficeth us. Jesus saith unto him, have I been so long time with you, and yet hast thou not known me, Philip? he that hath seen me hath seen the Father; and how sayest thou then, Show us the Father? Believest thou not that I am in the Father, and the Father in me? the words that I speak unto you I speak not of myself: but the Father that dwelleth in me, he doeth the works. Believe me that I am in the Father, and the Father in me: or else believe me for the very works' sake.* (John 14:8–11)

What is Jesus trying to convince people of by His works? He is saying that the works are the proof that He is in God. If you establish that Jesus is in God, then you will be in God. You can never be you trying to establish yourself. You can only establish you by allowing Him to be in you.

John 14:20 says, *At that day ye shall know that I am in my Father, and ye in me, and I in you.* That is what He is trying to get you to understand. He basically said, "It does not make a difference for you to be in Me, if you do not understand that I am in Him. You will never take advantage of Me being in you if you do not understand I am in Him. You will not understand the purpose of Me being in you, if you do not understand I am in Him. You think I am trying to do what I want to do, because that is what happened to you. You try to do what you want to do, but just as I deny Myself, you must deny yourself."

If you deny yourself and do not allow Jesus to be Himself, then denying yourself will not benefit anything. When you are just fasting and not spending time with Him and receiving His benefits from the fast, the only thing you are doing is dieting. There is a purpose for everything. There is a purpose for you not being you. It is for God to be God. If you do not let Him be Himself, or if the impression you are giving is not the Father, then any other impression is not right. You might as well be just you, somebody else, or anybody else.

John 14:28 says, *Ye have heard how I said unto you, I go away, and come again unto you. If ye loved me, ye would rejoice, because I said, I go unto the Father: for my Father is greater than I.* We have been lacking by not going to that place of sufficiency and the fullness of what God wanted to manifest which is acknowledging God the Father, God the Son, and God the Holy Spirit. We are not placing the Father, the Son, and the Holy Spirit in the proper order in our lives, with the proper importance and the proper purpose for our lives.

Think about these questions: Do you want God's best for your family? Do you want the fullness of what God has for you? If so, you must also follow the proper order God established for the family. Look at it in terms of establishing the proper order in your earthly family. One common strategy is that you can never put your child above your spouse, especially in blended families. It does not matter if they are your biological children or not; putting the children ahead of your spouse is a recipe for disaster. If divine order is not in place, the fullness of your family cannot be released.

Likewise, you can never put Jesus above the Father. This statement does not mean I am speaking against Jesus; I am speaking with what Jesus said Himself about Himself. Jesus said the Father is greater than He is. So why do you place Jesus above the Father? Please realize that God is going to release some greatness in you, but you have to know how to honor the Father with the greatness.

John 15:9–10 says, *As the Father hath loved me, so have I loved you: continue ye in my love. If ye keep my commandments, ye shall abide in my love; even as I have kept my Father's commandments, and abide in his love.* Jesus is the truth, the way, the path, and the bridge to the Father. When Jesus said for us to ask Him nothing else, we think He is saying it in the sense of asking for a need or provision. To a degree, we are correct in this understanding that we do not need to ask Him about our need or our provision, but there is a step further we have missed. Jesus does not want us to go to the Father and ask for needs or provision either. Jesus instructed us that just as He asks the Father for what He wants Him to do, Jesus wants us to go to the Father and ask Him what He wants us to do.

Jesus said and is saying to us today, "Just as He (God) told Me what He wanted me to do, let Him (God) tell you what He wants you to do. What God told me is for me, and I (Jesus) was an example for you. The works I (Jesus) do, shall you also do and do even greater works than what I did. These works are something He (God) told you. He did not tell me (Jesus). I did mine. Now you do yours." When you only follow the letter (Bible) and not allow the Spirit to lead you; you will start doing what Jesus did and not do what God tells you to do.

Can you imagine how some people would start spitting in the ground and rubbing mud in someone's eyes trying to heal the blind. But that is what He told Jesus to do. Jesus heard God the Father, He did it, and it worked. Now, what is God telling you to do to get the healing? You cannot do exactly what Jesus did. He got it from the Father. Jesus is not telling you to do what He tells you. He is telling you to go to the Father and find out what He wants.

You will never see the fullness and the maximum results of your life by just doing what was written. You can just do the "letter" and you are going to get some results. However, you are never going to get the fullness of what is for you. The written word cannot contain all of God. It cannot contain all of the explicit directions for your life. It can speak generally to your life, but what I am talking about are things specifically for you. Jesus (the Word) cannot tell you the specific word to tell your spouse, but the Father can. He can tell you specifically what to say.

The Bible cannot specifically tell you where to go, what to see, or who to talk to. Yet God the Father can specifically call you by name and tell you. This order works; just remember you will never get the fullness of it until you direct your focus toward God. Jesus did say go to the Father in His name, but still go to the Father. You know, Jesus deals with threes: outer court, inner court, and Holy of Holies. You can come to the outer court and get a residue. You can come to the inner court and get a little bit more. However, it is not until you get to the Holy of Holies that you will have it all.

Some people like to stay on the bridge and look over to the other side. You cannot be like the children of Israel when they first got to the Promise Land, standing on one side and looking over. You have to go and be a partaker of it. You have to go across. Jesus is the bridge, He is the path, and He is the way. You have to go beyond Jesus and get to the Father. I know you love Jesus and you should, but you can never get to the Father until you get to Jesus. Just do not let Jesus be your final dwelling place. *Jesus saith unto her, Touch me not; for I am not yet ascended to my Father: but go to my brethren, and say unto them, I ascend unto my Father, and your Father; and to my God, and your God* (John 20:17).

Jesus, the Word, is for our soul, our mind, and for reasoning. This Word provides the biggest benefit for us by convincing us to think more like God. It is to get us to change our perspective and our way of thinking so that it will line up with God's will and God's purpose for our lives. This is what the Bible does. It regulates our minds. There are not many places in the Old Testament of the Bible that mention the Father, yet it talks mostly about God. Even though the Bible is written this way, you know distinctly that it is talking about God the Father. In the Old Testament, He has not separated Himself. God was God the Father, God the Son, and God the Holy Spirit. He only begins to identify the separation in the New Testament, because the fullness of God came when Jesus was born.

The Issue of Sonship

This is one of the biggest issues that religion has. They do not believe Jesus is God's Son. If you cannot believe that, then you cannot be God's son. Notice the words stated in John 20:17 but go to my *Father and your Father, and to my God and to your God.* This is what I wanted to identify so that you can realize that He is just not Jesus' Father. I taught a message called "We are His children and He is our Father." The theme was, as long as you keep saying God and revere Him only as God, you will never connect to Him. He will become this awesome being sitting on this awesome throne who is untouchable to you. When you make Him your Father, He becomes the intimate and influential person. He becomes this person of provision, power, might, and love in your life.

It is not what He is in others, but who He is to you. He is *my* daddy. He is my Father, and because of that, I can go to Him. When you are still going by way of Jesus, you have acknowledged that He is Jesus' Father, but you have not accepted the fact that He is yours also.

It is just like in your family. Imagine you have three kids and the oldest child kept sending the youngest one to the parents to get permission. "Go ask Momma or Daddy if we can do this." What the parent really wants is for the oldest child to be able to come to them by himself. You do not, and should not, have to go through a third party just to interact and talk to your parents.

You should want that personal relationship, because you will never know them like they need to be known, and they will never know you like you need to be known. It will not happen until you have that personal relationship by spending time alone with them. So likewise, that is what God wants. The Father wants an intimate and personal one-on-one relationship just with you. He does not want you to communicate to Him through your big brother Jesus. God says, "Jesus did what I wanted Him to do. He did it so that you can do what I want you to do. However, you have to come to me. I am not giving it to Him. I am giving it to you. You have to do it."

This intimate and personal relationship with the Father will help us to completely realize the importance of what we do. For example, most churches have praise and worship service before the word goes forth. The original intent was to prepare members for the word. How many of you do that on your own? Most people just open up their Bible and start reading, not realizing that they have not prepared themselves to read. Why? It is because they have now exalted the reading above the relationship. The reading is only to take you to the relationship.

Reading the Bible is not a substitute for God's presence. You are not going to understand what you read as well as what you should read without the relationship. Without the relationship, you are not going to have the one who is going to speak to you directly through what you read. Some may say, "Well, I've got the Holy Spirit." This way of thinking will be discussed in greater detail later in the book where we talk about His part; but for now I just want to clarify the role of the Spirit. The Holy Spirit is not an errand boy. He will not be a substitute for one's slothfulness in establishing a relationship with the Father. The Holy Spirit is only a helper. He will not do what you can do, and He will not do what you have been created to do. He will only assist you in doing it. If you are not doing it first, He cannot help you.

Head Knowledge vs. Heart Knowledge

Most Christians have more word in their "knowing head" than they are ever going to be able to do with that knowledge. Some can quote scriptures better than the pastor can. However, it is not important to see how many scriptures the pastor can quote, but what *is* impressive is how many scriptures he can live by. As a pastor, it does not mean anything for me to know all of the scriptures, but not to live any of them. It is like when people need to give, they know they need to give, and the Bible says they need to give, but still they do not.

When believers need to be kind, forgive, or repent, they know they need to, and the Bible says they need to, but still they do not.

When they need to come into a place of unity with their brother, they know that, but they still are not doing it. What sense does it make for me to know it when I am not doing it? I would rather for you to know less scripture, and do more of what you know than to have you to know many scriptures and not do any of it.

This behavior is what the Bible calls being like sounding brass and tinkling cymbal, having a form and denying the power (1 Corinthians 13:1; 2 Timothy 3:5). Is it the word by itself that makes us successful and produce good fruit? Many people have been in church for a long time; they know a lot of God's word, and they are submitted to good, anointed, appointed blessed women and men of God. Yet look closely in comparison to that, and ask yourself, how much of your life has changed? If you have not changed, then what was the hindrance?

> *And he taught them many things by parables, and said unto them in his doctrine, Hearken; Behold, there went out a sower to sow: And it came to pass, as he sowed, some fell by the way side, and the fowls of the air came and devoured it up. And some fell on stony ground, where it had not much earth; and immediately it sprang up, because it had no depth of earth: But when the sun was up, it was scorched; and because it had no root, it withered away. And some fell among thorns, and the thorns grew up, and choked it, and it yielded no fruit.* (Mark 4:2–7)

Notice that the sower sowed seeds on different types of ground, or soil today would be soil. According to the parable, was the outcome of what was not produced based on the seed? No. It is based on the ground. What happened to the seed was based on the ground, not the seed. It was the same seed, but different conditions of ground. *And other fell on good ground, and did yield fruit that sprung up and increased; and brought forth, some thirty, and some sixty, and some an hundred. And he said unto them, Know ye not this parable? and how then will ye know all parables? The sower soweth the word* (Mark 4:8, 13–14 KJV).

So then in order to get a good harvest in our lives, do we need to sow some more words? No. Mark 4:15 says, *And these are they by the way side, where the word is sown; but when they have heard, Satan cometh immediately, and taketh away the word that was sown in their hearts.* We have to pay attention to the ground. It is not the word that produces, because what can limit the word? It is limited by the ground, and the ground where the seed of God's word is planted is in your heart.

The spirit man is your heart that is developed by your intimate, personal one-on-one relationship with the Father. That is why you have praise service before the word goes forth. Through worship, you can develop an intimate one-on-one relationship with the Father which helps your heart to be good soil for the seed of God's word. Even though a church service can be full of people who hear the same word of God, we will get many different results. It is not because the word is different. It is because of the different conditions of people's heart that it fell on. What determines the type of heart you possess and ultimately what happens to the word? It is your relationship with him, the Father, or a lack thereof.

Draw Near to God and He Will Draw Near to You

If you have ever planted a garden, then you know that you cannot put the seed in the ground and then prepare the ground afterward. No, you prepare the ground and get it ready for the seed, and then you sow the seed. It is no different with the seed of the word of God. You must first go and get your heart right. You get it ready through an intimate relationship. You can read the Bible all day long, but what makes His word become real to you? Sometimes you are not going to find that certain scripture. You have to hear that scripture first and then you should decide to look for it. He is going to talk to you, which is going to open up your heart so that the scripture can have a place in it.

On the other hand, what if you do not ever talk to Him? What if you do not ever go to Him and develop any type of relationship with Him so that He can speak clearly, precisely, and directly to you? There are things that only you and He can talk about, things that only you and He know, and directions that only He can tell you. Once you decide to spend time with Him, nobody else can draw Him away from you. Nobody else can convince you that He is not real and that He cannot do anything for you. Nobody else can convince you that He does not love you, especially when He talks to you specifically.

Do not get me wrong. It is still good and necessary for believers to come to church and hear God's word being preached. However, I am not just talking about what He says to and through pastors. I am talking about the things He tells you directly that flesh and blood have not revealed unto you but your Father. Moreover, the gates of hell shall not prevail against it (Matthew 16:17–18). It is because when you hear it for yourself, you are secure. Nobody can tell you He did not say it. You did not hear it through a third party. One of His other children did not come and tell you what He said. He told you face to face. It is time to experience the Father's love, and you cannot do that through anyone else. You can only do that with an intimate personal relationship with Him.

The Keys to the Kingdom

In times past, believers have never fully taken advantage of the word that we have received to the point that it had the full effect on our lives in what we do. In some way, form, or fashion, we are partly hearers of the word and not fully doers of the word. We are living in such a day and time that believing and acting according to the word is very essential. Believers should start believing and doing the things that we believe. As we do that which we believe, we will start manifesting that which is supposed to be manifested. Without that, there is no hope.

If believers cannot produce the word that we say we believe, what hope does the world have? If we cannot allow the light to shine in our darkness, then what hope does the world have? If we cannot get answers to our prayers, then what hope does the world have? Since we are the salt of the earth and the light of the world, we must become what we want them to become. This is in order for them to believe that they can be what they want to become. The Bible says, *I've given unto you keys to the kingdom* (Matthew 16:19). Thus, we take the keys, we use the keys, we get results, and then we acquire additional keys.

All of you should know that God has more keys, which means He has more word. Thus, He has more things He wants to give you. It does not matter if you have been living on the earth and have been saved for one hundred years; there is still more of God that He wants to give you. There is more understanding, more revelation, more ability, more anointing, and more power that He wants to release in your life. This fact is what you must understand. He has more keys! However, what most people do is since He has more keys, they get rid of the keys they already have.

The keys I am referring to are revelation (revealed knowledge and wisdom). Believers exchange their keys instead of adding to what they already have. You may have something different, but you are no better than you were because you do not have more than you had. What He wants you to do is keep the keys you have, put them together along with the new keys He gives you and be better.

Remember, I am not lessening the importance of Jesus. I am just putting the Father in His place. Unfortunately, what many people are doing now is replacing Jesus with the Father. Many people have a solid relationship with Jesus who is in their life.

However, once they learned they did not have the Father, they unconsciously put down Jesus and picked up the Father. I am not asking you to put down Jesus, or put less emphasis on Jesus. I am saying to put a greater emphasis on the Father.

When you put a greater emphasis on the Father, Jesus will have a greater impact, effect, and place in your life. 2 Timothy 2:15 says, *Study to shew thyself approved unto God, a workman that needeth not to be ashamed, rightly dividing the word of truth.* I have never wanted and will never desire for you to put my word above God's word. I want you to study the word of God for yourself and put it in the place that He wants it to be in your life.

Different Levels

When you deal with people, you can find that they are at different levels and aspects. Some are in the beginning stages of maturity in Christ, some are midway, while some are coming into the fullness of knowing who God is and who they are supposed to be. You will need to find out where you are and put whatever you need in your life as He reveals it to you. Everything God has for you may not belong to you at this time, but if you endure long enough, you will receive everything for your life.

Keep in mind that you must be open to change. I believe sometimes we resist change in our lives because we are afraid of what may happen. We are afraid to venture out into something else other than what our tradition has made us accustomed to. What is tradition? Is it doing something repeatedly? That is not necessarily tradition. In general the word *tradition* means *the transmission of customs or beliefs from generation to generation.* Theologically speaking, tradition is a *doctrine believed to have divine authority though not in the scriptures.* However, tradition is when you take something and do it over and over again without a purpose or an understanding of why you are doing it. Consequently, this form of tradition has made the word of God of no effect in our lives. There are some things you need to do over and over again, but if you do not understand why you are doing it and do not know the purpose of doing it, then it can become tradition, and therefore it has no effect.

You hear the word and pray, but why do you pray? Furthermore, why do you pray in Jesus' name? I think it is out of tradition, but what is the purpose? The Bible says when you pray in the name of Jesus, every demon will tremble. How many demons are trembling at you when you call out the name of Jesus? It may not be many if you are doing it out of tradition without a purpose and an understanding. Therefore, now you are making the word of

God of no effect. I do not want you to be an individual or a part of the body of Christ that is receiving the word of God but getting no effect. Again, I would rather you receive a little of the word of God and get a lot of effect on that little word than to receive a lot of the word of God and not get any effect.

You have received a lot of word. You know a lot of word, but where does it fit in your life? What effects are you seeing? You have to change. You have to be made better. You have to do something greater. You have to be conformed to a better image that is not your image, the world's image, or anybody else's image. It has to be God's image. You have to see that you are becoming more like Him in the way you speak, think, respond, act, and in the way you are. If that is not the case, then what is the use of the word? What is the purpose of the word? Why did Jesus die, and why do you come to church? Why were you saved?

If this word seems a little intense, then it is because of my compassion. No one is perfect. Perfection is a destiny that everyone should be striving to reach. Personally, I try to walk in a spirit of excellence. I always try to get better, to excel, to improve, to be consistent with my life, and to live what I speak. That which I speak is what I believe. This is what I try to do. I try to allow people to see my life, as well as the consistency of God in my life.

That is what you should strive for. Every day there is a better vision of who God is in you than there was the day before. If you are still going through the same tradition, you know what, we will be here next year talking about the same old thing. Some of you may need a new church, a new start, or a new beginning. Old things are passed away. You can never get out of the shadow of who you were being in the same place. God will give you an opportunity to come into a new place to be judged, not on whom you were, but on who you are becoming. However, if your reflection is the same old reflection as before, there will not be any difference in you. If your actions are the same old actions, then there will not be any difference in your actions. This is a new day, a new hour, and God is doing a new thing.

This may be a challenging book to read for some, but what I just said was the truth, the whole truth, and nothing but the truth. I take the word of God very seriously. I take the changes in people's lives very seriously. It does you no good to hear a word and not change, especially when you have the capability of changing. You would then be judged even more harshly because of what you know, *for to whom much is given, much is required* (Luke 12:48).

I would rather for you to just stay ignorant and not know and let things happen than for you to know and refuse to do what you do know. Sure enough, things will happen. Jesus felt the same way, and for this reason Jesus spared people. Jesus said, "You know there are a lot of things I want to tell you, but you aren't ready to receive it." It was not as if they were not going to understand it or be able to hear it. It was just that they were not ready to do it. Since they were not ready to do it, He said that He was not going to tell them because it would not be an advantage but a disadvantage for them.

In this day and time, we are not average people doing average things. We are supernatural people doing supernatural things, because we have the supernatural ability of God. God has required us to walk in that supernatural ability in which we have the understanding, the revelation, and the anointing to walk in. We have everything it takes, so now we just have to decide to do it. I realize this book may challenge some of your old ways of thinking. It is not to take things away from you, but to add a better piece to you.

The Father's Heart

In the book of John, God reveals the love affair that He expressed that Jesus had toward the Father God. Since He reveals such a love connection in the book of John like no other book in the Bible, I think that this is the Father's heart. Being in love with God to the degree that the connection is so strong we can hear and obey what He says without doubt or hesitation like Jesus did, is the heart that God wants us as children of His to operate in.

Again, 1 Thessalonians 5:23 says, *And the very God of peace sanctify you wholly; and I pray God your whole spirit and soul and body be preserved blameless unto the coming of our Lord Jesus Christ.* I want to reiterate that we are a spirit who possess a soul and live in a body, just as God is a triune God—God the Father, God the Son, and God the Holy Spirit. As I mentioned before, these three parts of God develop different parts of man. Also, the relationship has to be in the right order in order to maximize the development. I am not saying that you cannot be general in the things of God and not see results, but it works best in the appropriate order.

Are you not tired of what you have in comparison to what God has for you and what God wants you to walk in and to live in? Many of us are merely eating crumbs from the table, but we are not sitting at the table.

Jesus said, *The works that I do shall he do also; greater works than these shall he do* (John 14:12). Have you raised anybody from the dead? Have you opened up the blinded eyes of someone? Have you walked on water? Have you fed thousands of people with a two-piece fish dinner? How many of you have done any of these things? These are the works that Jesus did, and keep in mind He said greater works than these we shall do. We should not be doing less than Jesus did. We should be doing more. Why are we not doing it? It is because we are not maximizing our anointing. I am not saying we are not getting results. We are just not maximizing the results that we have the capability of getting.

How are we going to do that? We maximize our results by doing it in order, the right way, and being more specific. It is just like firing a shotgun. We can fire a shotgun, and the farther away we are from the target, the more scattered the pattern is going to be. If you shoot at an animal when you are so far from it and miss, you are only going to make it angrier. However, when you have a high-powered rifle, with a scope on it, you can pinpoint what you want to shoot, shoot it accurately, and hit the bulls-eye! That is what God wants us to do. God does not want us to stumble into anything. He does not want us to have any blunders of faith or accidents. For many believers, this is how things happen, and sometimes we have no understanding or knowledge of how the manifestation happened.

We get manifestations in this manner, but we cannot share with others how to make results happen in their lives because we do not know why it happened in ours. It just happened. There was a result, but it was not specific enough to make us proficient in our faith that we could hit it each and every time. Some people are still dealing with the same situations in their lives. Even if they get a rest from their issue for a little while, they end up back in it later on. Personally, I believe that I do not have to go through the same things repeatedly. Once I go through it and if I am more specific about what happened, then I should learn the lesson well enough to not deal with it again.

When will you understand what is going on to the point that you can stop it? When will you understand well enough what is going on and the attacks and the tricks of the enemy that you know what needs to happen through you to keep it from happening again? Success is not things changing to conform to what you want. The devil is not going to ever change to be what you want him to be. However, you can change to where he does not have any effect on you.

You are looking at everything around you to change, instead of looking at what is *in* you to change you. Understanding this concept is what is going to develop you to change. You cannot affect everything around you until you affect everything *in* you. Until that which is in you has been affected, you will not have influence over things of this earth.

His Purpose Despite the Problems

And he that searcheth the hearts knoweth what is the mind of the Spirit, because he maketh intercession for the saints according to the will of God. And we know that all things work together for good to them that love God, to them who are the called according to his purpose. (Romans 8:27–28)

This scripture helps you to understand that in everything God has a purpose, and realize that it does not matter what is coming at you. All things work together for your good. Not everything may be good, yet I know that the outcome of it is going to be good. He said in His word, *In the world ye shall have tribulation: but be of good cheer; I have overcome the world* (John 16:33).

He also said, *Think it not strange concerning the fiery trial which is to try you, as though some strange thing happened unto you* (1 Peter 4:12).

You are going to have some problems. You are going to have some trouble, but just because the trouble comes to you, it does not mean the trouble should overcome you. When you realize this fact, you will know that if God is for you then who can be against you? At this point, some of you may say, "I know what the Bible says. I know that if God be for me, who would be against me, but I also know what I did." If these are your thoughts, you do not know the Father's love. You know Him as God, but not as Father.

For those of you who are parents, what can your child do that will cause you to reject them? Even though you know they have done some things that are wrong, they are still your children. You are still going to love them, and whatever you can do to help them, you are going to do it. Now, you may be limited as to how you can help, and sometimes we limit God this way; however, there is never a lack of desire, wanting, and longing to help them.

This is why God sent His son Jesus so that you would have hope. If you are so consumed by the guilt of what you did, then you are in a place where Jesus cannot get to you, the place of indecision. You have not decided to let Jesus *be* in you. He will not take over. He will not make you nor force you to let Him in. If you ask, He will. If you yield, He can.

> *For whom he did foreknow, he also did predestinate to be conformed to the image of his Son, that he might be the firstborn among many brethren.* (Romans 8:29)

If Jesus is the "firstborn" of many brethren, then who are the rest of "many brethren"? Since Jesus is the son of God and the firstborn of many brethren, then that makes us children of God; thus He is our Father too! Realize this and take the journey to a place that is going to give you an awakening. You will see the desire of the Father who wants to show you who you really are. We have to get God off that throne in heaven where He has been perceived as being this "all-supreme" God looking to judge and condemn. We must make Him our heavenly Father who is concerned about His children and who loves every aspect of them in spite of the right and the wrong things that they do. He only desires the very best for His children.

Most of us, if not all of us, have had some form of parenting, whether it were good or bad. Even if you had bad parents, at least you should have learned what not to do. Yet God's goodness is the standard for all goodness. There is a longing as a born-again believer for the goodness to be manifested and revealed to us. We long for it, we crave for it, we thirst for it, and we hunger and seek after it.

Regardless of whether you had a good example or not of a parent, the God in you is longing for the goodness of God in Him. There is a craving in you. You know what is good from evil. You know right from wrong. You know God from the devil. This is because the spirit witnesses with only the truth. Even if you did not have good examples of parents, you can still recognize a good father when you see one. You just need to see and meet Him to satisfy that longing.

We allow our kids, spouse, and everything else to try to fulfill that longing. However, the longing that you are seeking can only be fulfilled by any substitute, not even by His son or His spirit. It can only be fulfilled by God, the Father, a substitute will not do. As I mentioned earlier in this chapter, what was disturbed, broken, and taken in the Garden of Eden was the relationship that Adam had with the Father (Genesis 1–3). However, even after the sin of Adam and Eve, even before Jesus came, there was still a relationship with the word. How could Abraham do what he did if he did not hear God's word? There was also still a relationship with the Spirit. How could Elijah outrun the chariot, if there was not the Spirit on him to do it?

With all of that, something was still lacking. It was the relationship with the Father. They could not get to that place of holiness: the Holy of Holies. There was still a veil they could not get behind. The Old Testament saints did not have that intimate personal relationship with God.

Thus, there is the significance of Jesus being the firstborn of many brethren. A relationship with the Father is impossible without understanding and accepting the condition in John 3. You have to be born-again to be a brethren.

> *Jesus answered and said unto him, Verily, verily, I say unto thee, Except a man be born again, he cannot see the kingdom of God. Nicodemus saith unto him, How can a man be born when he is old? Can he enter the second time into his mother's womb, and be born? Jesus answered, Verily, verily, I say unto thee, Except a man be born of water and of the Spirit, he cannot enter into the kingdom of God. That which is born of the flesh is flesh; and that which is born of the Spirit is spirit.* (John 3:3–6)

He is not talking about your flesh being born-again. He is talking about your spirit being born-again, because the spirit is the real you.

Embrace Your Place and Responsibility

> *And seeing the multitudes, he went up into a mountain: and when he was set, his disciples came unto him: And he opened his mouth, and taught them, saying, Blessed are the poor in spirit: for theirs is the kingdom of heaven.* (Matthew 5:1–3)

We misunderstood this scripture totally. Let us read further. Matthew 5:4–5 says, *Blessed are they that mourn: for they shall be comforted. Blessed are the meek: for they shall inherit the earth.* It is not the high-minded, not the arrogant, not the pompous who inherit the earth, but the meek. When you are trying to take the high-minded road instead of yielding, something is wrong. It is as if you are trying to make room for your gift, rather than letting your gift make room for you. If you have been called to do it, then you are going to do it. Why are you forcing something that is already God's will, which by the way cannot be stopped by anything? You have to let patience have her perfect work (James 1:4).

When you understand your relationship with the Father, what He wants for you cannot be stopped by anybody. The only person that can stop what God wants for you is you. If you are not going to stop it, it is not going to be stopped! Nobody can stop what God has for you. Nobody can stop God's destiny for you, but you!

You may say, "Well, it seems like I have been at this a long time." Well, that may be because most of the time, you have been the hindrance. *Blessed are they which do hunger and thirst after righteousness: for they shall be filled. Blessed are the merciful: for they shall obtain mercy. Blessed are the pure in heart: for they shall see God* (Matthew 5:6–8).

Jesus said *blessed,* and then He gives something that may seem not to be a blessing. Blessed are the poor in spirit, blessed are they that mourn, blessed are the meek, blessed are they that do hunger. In the second part of each verse, he gives the anecdote or the provision. *"Blessed are the poor in spirit for theirs is the kingdom of heaven."* This means if you are poor (lacking) in spirit, you have not received the kingdom of heaven. If He is my Father, this is His kingdom, and if I am His child, then it is my kingdom also! *Thy kingdom come, Thy will be done in earth, as it is in heaven.* (Matthew 6:10). When you do not receive Him or only see Him just as God, then you are seeing it as only His kingdom. It has nothing to do with you, because you don't receive it as your kingdom. That is why you stay poor in the spirit. The fullness and healthiness of your spirit is based on you receiving your sonship or your placement in the heavenly kingdom. God is your Father; therefore, you are an heir, or joint-heir with Christ Jesus (Galatians 4:7). *Blessed are the pure at heart for they shall see God. Blessed are the peacemakers for they shall be called the sons of God.* Is that you? Are you a peacemaker, or are you looking to stir up something? Judge yourself. You cannot be a child of God stirring up stuff. Are you willing to be a peacemaker? If so, then you cannot go around causing problems, stirring up trouble, and keeping contention among the people. You should be asking yourself, How can I solve this, not How can I make it worse? How can I make this smaller, not How can I make it bigger?

> *Blessed are they which are persecuted for righteousness' sake: for theirs is the kingdom of heaven. Blessed are ye, when men shall revile you, and persecute you, and shall say all manner of evil against you falsely, for my sake. Rejoice, and be exceeding glad: for great is your reward in heaven: for so persecuted they the prophets which were before you.* (Matthew 5:10–12)

> *Ye are the salt of the earth: but if the salt have lost his savour, wherewith shall it be salted? It is thenceforth good for nothing, but to be cast out, and to be trodden under foot of men. Ye are the light of the world. A city that is set on an hill cannot be hid. Neither do men light a candle, and put it under a bushel, but on a candlestick; and it giveth light unto all that are in the house. Let your light so shine before men, that they may see your good works, and glorify your Father which is in heaven.* (Matthew 5:13–16)

The light, the works, the salt, and the effects are what the world needs to be a partaker of Him in you. You cannot do that if you are not glorifying your Father. It is not what you do, it is who He is in you. Earlier, I mentioned the word tradition and what makes it a tradition. You can do many things in tradition, but tradition is when you do not have the understanding or the knowledge of what you do, but you still do it. When you do things that could give Him the glory, and since people do not understand the purpose and the reason for doing it, they do not give Him the glory. Therefore, you did the works, but He was not glorified in it.

This is the point where you start taking credit for what has been done. Then you start looking more at you for what you do, but less of Him and who He is in you. Now, you want people to see you and not Him. You do not know you are only a reflection of who He is and without Him you can do nothing.

Let us go back to *blessed are the peacemakers.* When we look at the word *peacemaker,* we think tranquility, calmness, or no disruption. It also means provision being provided for. As I mentioned earlier peace is shalom, which means nothing missing, nothing broken, and nothing lacking. When you are a peacemaker, you bring nothing broken and nothing lacking to the situation. If you bring whatever is lacking (to a solution), if you bring whatever is missing (for a solution), and if you provide whatever is needed, then you become a peacemaker.

Also, when an issue does not have the flavor of God, you become the salt. If there is a situation that does not reflect Him and when you come, you bring Him, now you reflect who He is in the situation. So are you the peacemaker, or do you bring the devil? I am not trying to be harsh, but I am merely stating a fact. If you are not bringing the God in you, then you are bringing the devil. If you are not helping, you are hurting. If you are not adding, you are taking away.

In Romans 1:7 Paul wrote, *To all that be in Rome, beloved of God, called to be saints: Grace to you and peace from God our Father, and the Lord Jesus Christ.* If you are a peacemaker, you get your peace from God, God our Father and the Lord Jesus Christ. One of the things I noticed in this scripture is the separation between peace of our God and Father and Lord Jesus Christ. The early church had a distinct separation of the Father and Jesus, but today for some reason, we do not. We have made our relationship so common that we lump the Trinity together. We do not see the full effect of each part of God like they did.

Do you now know and understand that He is our Father? Will you receive Him as your Father, and not just God Almighty? He is that, but He is so much more. He is God Almighty to everybody, but He is not Father to everyone. Everyone has not accepted Jesus and been born-again into the family of the Father. He is God, but He is more than that to us. He is God to the sinners. He was God before you were saved. However, once you became saved, He became your Father.

Would you do more for someone else's kids before you do for your own? Would you want more for someone else's kids than you want more for your own? Would you lump other kids in the same category as your own? No, you would not, and neither does God. Do you not know He prizes you above those that do not accept Him as Father? I am not saying that He loves you more, but that there is more provision already in place for you because you have accepted Him.

The kingdom is for you. It is for them too (those who only see Him as God) once they have accepted Him. Unfortunately, it is not for them when they do not choose Him. God is a purposeful God. Do you wonder why there is a lot of lack in many area of people's lives? It is because lack has nothing to do with anything other than who is your source or who is your provider. Since God the Father is your provider, lack is eliminated in every aspect regardless of where it is, who it is, or how it is. Even in the most desolate place, God can still become a source and cause you to prosper.

You cannot do it on your own, and your circumstances will not do it on its own. As children of God, He wants to make your dry land a prosperous land. He wants to make any lack in your life full of abundance. You cannot do that by categorizing Him as just God. He is God for everybody, yet everybody is not getting their needs met by Him. Everybody will not have access to His resources, but He will give access to His children. As His child, He has provided for you. His son died for you so that you may be His sons and daughters. You are not in the same category as this world.

So separate yourself and do not do or think that you are subject to what they are subject to.

You do not have to endure what they endure. You do not have to put up with what they have to put up with. You are not in their class. You see Him as Father and you do not just see Him as God. The difference is not just God alone, because most religions honor and worship some form of God. The difference is what position Jesus has in you. When you start talking about Jesus being the Son of God, you will know you have the difference with other religions. The benefit of Jesus being the Son of God is that we can be the sons and daughters of God through him.

As Jesus is the partaker, so are we. As God did it for Him, so He can and will do it for us. That is the difference. Again, you lessen His effect when you lump Him all together and do not identify Jesus as the Son. Making Him the Son of God benefits you more than just making Him God. I emphatically reiterate, when He becomes the Son of God and you are born into the family, then you become the son of God. The things He walks in, you can too. However, if He is just God, then God can walk in anything, but you cannot. Therefore, it greatly benefits us separating them (the Trinity).

Concluding Chapter 1

I have explained why being specific in our development is so very important and how we do it is to recognize that each part of God develops a different part of man. The primary part of man is man's spirit. God's spirit is in your spirit. Our spirit is developed by our intimate personal one-on-one relationship with the Father and there is no substitute for that. Even our relationship with Jesus is not a substitute for our relationship with the Father. Jesus came to be a bridge to the Father and not to replace Him. He came to show you and lead you to the Father. As I stated earlier, I am not telling you to get rid of Jesus. I am saying you are never going to receive the full benefit of Jesus until you know the Father.

You will never know why the Father sent Jesus unless you get to know the Father. You will never know the love that the Father has for you. Until you get to know Him, you will never know why He loved you so much that He sent His only begotten Son to die for you. Jesus was not sent here to benefit our spirit even though He can. Yet, that is not the primary reason for Him coming, staying, or the primary reason for the word. The word is not to develop your spirit, but the word is to develop your mind. The scripture states, *Let this mind be in you; and the Word became flesh* (Philippians 2:5; John 1:14).

The word is to change how you think. It is to change your decision-making ability. This is the only reason for which Jesus came. Jesus came to change and give man another perspective of choice. Once man made the choice, his spirit was changed. Regrettably, what we usually cater to is always to the lesser. I am not talking about Jesus being less, yet in comparison to the Father, Jesus said, *My Father is greater than I* (John 14:28). Jesus said, *I do not do anything than what the Father tells me* (John 8:28). He said He did not come to testify of Himself. He came to testify of Him who sent Him.

There are some things even lesser than Jesus that we cater to and are drawn to, which is the Spirit of God. That is why you always see people coming in hundreds and thousands for these miracles. Conversely, you cannot seek the miracle without seeking the one who is the author of it. If so, you will not keep the effects of the miracle. If you receive a miracle today without any understanding, then you are going to need another miracle tomorrow. That is the truth. God never intended for us to live by miracles. Miracles were never intended for believers. Miracles are for those who do not believe so that they might believe.

It is a fact and it saddens me to say that we always flock to the "lesser." We want that anointing on our body and it is the Spirit of God who is sent for our flesh. In Acts 2:17 he said, *And it shall come to pass in the last days, saith God, I will pour out of my Spirit upon all flesh.*

This statement is referring to the super ability on that natural body to give you supernatural ability to do what you could not do before the Spirit of God came upon you. That is what we want. The problem is that we want to get that supernatural ability without getting some understanding. The understanding is the Word, which is Jesus. Then we want to get understanding without getting the relationship, and we cannot do that. Please do not misunderstand that I am not lessening any of part or function of the Trinity. I must reiterate that once you get a relationship, you will get the understanding, and once you get the understanding, you will have some anointing. It is out of order when we want the anointing before we get the understanding, and then we want the understanding before we get the relationship. This is just like the cart pulling the horse, or the tail wagging the dog.

Let us still establish the fact that the spirit man is developed by the relationship with the Father. You must put emphasis on your relationship with the Father. Again, we waste time in prayer because we do not know the importance of the relationship with the Father. Let me reiterate this point by sharing about my relationship with my natural parents, and the relationship I had with my father and how good it was. It taught me how to appreciate the things he did. When I did not have the relationship, I did not appreciate the things he did for me, even though he did many things. It was not until I established a relationship with my natural father that it made me more appreciative of who he was and how he lived.

So likewise, God the Father has done so many things for you, yet you will never be appreciative of Him until you learn appreciation by way of the relationship with Him. Once you learn through the relationship, then an act as simple as getting up in the morning is a blessing. However, when you do not have a relationship, you sometimes misuse the advantage that you have. On the other hand, when you have that relationship and you cultivate that relationship, you develop a stronger relationship. You do not waste your time.

When you establish that relationship with God, then the word that you do know will have greater meaning. It is not because of the word being changed, but because the relationship with the Father has changed. I know who He is and the love that He has toward me. Remember the keys that he gave you to the kingdom? Well, I do not want you to change keys. I want you to add more keys to your key ring. Let us continue to do so in the succeeding chapter.

CHAPTER 2

The Son Jesus—Developing the Mind

God is a good God, and I am going to keep on reminding you of that. Circumstances and situations may not remind you of how good our God is. People may not remind you of that either. However, God is still a good God. His goodness is not based on situations or circumstances.

Developing the Complete You is a revelation that God gave to me concerning how to maximize our potential by maximizing His effects on us. Remember, 1 Thessalonians 5:23 says, *And the very God of peace sanctify you wholly.*

Peace means shalom: nothing missing, nothing broken, and nothing lacking. When you have peace in God, it means that there's nothing missing, broken, or lacking in your life. God is your source, and He is your all sufficiency.

The very God of peace will sanctify you. It will set you apart, separate, or bring you unto Him. You cannot separate something until you bring it from something to something else. One of the issues that we have as the body of Christ is that we are trying to get rid of something, without replacing it with something else. Ironically, there has never been a void in your life because there is always something occupying your space. If it is not light, then it is darkness. If it is not darkness, it is light. No matter how you look at it, there is not a void in your space. You just do not know what's occupying your space.

Therefore, God wants to sanctify you. He wants to separate you from the "world," and He wants to bring you to Him. If you come from the "world" and do not go to Him, you may go back to the "world" and it will turn out worse than how you came from it. This is why I do not believe in casual casting out of devils. As believers, we have the ability and authority to cast out devils (Matthew 7:22; 10:8; Mark 1:39; 3:15; 6:13; and 16:17; Luke 11:20). We have authority over the evil one, the wicked one, but if that person does not want the devil to be gone, leave that devil alone.

When you cast the devil out of a person who really does not want that devil to be gone, the demon will go and find some of his buddies. He will come back and that person will be worse than he was before you cast it out (Matthew 12:43–45). Just leave the devil in there and bind him up. When you bind him, you render him useless in his effect on you. He still can work through that individual, but he cannot work toward you.

So this is the desired goal for you according to 1 Thessalonians 5:23, which states, *And I pray God your whole spirit and soul and body be preserved blameless unto the coming of our Lord Jesus Christ.*

The Three Parts of Man

As we discussed earlier, man is a spirit who possesses a soul and lives in a body, so there are the three parts of man. The primary part of you is your spirit. Your whole spirit, soul, and body should be preserved blameless until the coming of our Lord Jesus Christ. Remember we were made after the image of God because He said, "I will make man after my likeness and in our image." Therefore, we are a triune being just as God is a triune God. He is God the Father, God the Son, and God the Holy Spirit.

1 John 5:7 says, *For there are three that bear record in heaven, the Father, the Word, and the Holy Ghost: and these three are one.*

Jesus and the word are the same. Jesus, the word and the Son are one and the same (John 1:1, 14). Thus, the Father, the word, and the Holy Ghost are the same, which is the triune part of God. He is God the Father, God the Son, and God the Holy Ghost.

Man is a spirit who possesses a soul but lives in a body. Each part of God develops a different part of man. As chapter 1 illustrated, our spirit man, which is the primary part of us, is developed by an intimate personal one-on-one relationship with the Father. There is no substitute for an intimate personal relationship with the Father. Our mind, our soul, our thinker, our chooser, our feeler is developed by Jesus the word, the Son. Our flesh, our body, is developed by the Spirit of God. He said, *I will pour out of my spirit on all flesh* (Acts 2:17).

This gives you that supernatural ability to do that which you could not do before He came on you. Each part of God develops a different part of man, and that is how we maximize the fullness of man.

Again, we must put emphasis on the primary part, the Father's relationship since this is what was broken in the garden. God desires and longs to have an intimate, personal relationship with you. Many people in church hear the same word, but the results vary from person to person. It is not because the word is different. It is because your relationship with the Father is different.

You will never maximize the potential that the word has in your life until you start emphasizing the relationship you have with the Father. Keep in mind the example of a set of keys in your hand. I do not want you to take the keys that you have and replace them with the keys you are getting. I want you to add the keys that you receive along with the keys that you already have. This is not a substitute.

We always, for the most part, acknowledge and have a relationship with Jesus. Yet Jesus is the way. Jesus is the door. Jesus is the bridge and the path. If you do not know where He is leading you and go there, you will never benefit or fully maximize His potential. He is trying to lead you to the Father. I am not telling you to forget about Jesus. You will never get to the Father without Jesus. I am saying keep the same zeal, the same fervency, and the same excitement you have for Jesus. Those are the keys you have. In addition, add that desire, longing, and love for the Father, then you will now see how much of a benefit Jesus really is. In this chapter we will discuss more in depth on the Son, Jesus and how He will develop our mind.

Jesus Developing the Mind

Your mind and your soul are one and the same. Your soul and your mind are your thinker, your feeler, and your chooser. It is your reasoning, emotions, and understanding. All of these things are wrapped up in your soul which is in your mind. This is the pinnacle where we win or lose it. The mind is where the battlefield is. Based on your thinker, feeler, and chooser, you can either go toward the flesh or go toward the spirit. We can somewhat get beyond the flesh, but once we get to the mind's way of thinking, it will either take us back to the flesh or over to the spirit. This is where we have to make the difference.

We are going to begin by establishing Jesus, the Son, and the word as the same. Keep in mind that your soul and mind are your thinker, your feeler, your reasoning, your emotions, and your understanding. Many times in the Old Testament, there was no separation of the spirit and the soul. There was also no separation of the Father and the Son. As we get into the New Testament, we need to begin to be more specific and direct. As we grow in the things of God, the path does not get broader; it gets narrower, more specific, and less generic. We must begin to be more specific in what we are doing and in what we are attempting to accomplish in our lives.

We can make decisions and do things that we think are best for us. However, if we do not know the direction to take, we will not know how to judge what is being done. Here is an example to help describe your life. If you want to go to Miami, Florida, from Georgia, you must get on Interstate 75 South. If you get on Interstate 75 North, will that lead you to where you want to go? Even though you are on the right Interstate, you are going in the wrong direction. Again, if we do not know the specific location or destination that we are trying to get to, then we will not know how to judge the path, or the steps of God in our lives.

If we cannot judge the path correctly, we end up making costly mistakes. For instance, you cannot tell me that God called you to be a part of a church in Georgia, yet you accept a job in California. The step that He is leading you to does not line up with the path and the purpose you are taking in your life. When you understand the purpose, you can judge the steps. When you do not understand the purpose, you will try different things. This is the result of simply generalizing an action instead of being specific.

You may think a decision worked for someone else, and now you want to see if it will work for you. What you do not understand is that this is what God told them to do. You have to ask yourself, what is God telling me to do? It is not what you do, but it is what He *tells* you to do that will work. This is getting the specific word for your life and not generalizing God's word for your life. Why get specific? You have to go to God and ask Him what He wants for you and not listen to what He is doing for others. He wants that personal, intimate relationship with you.

John 1:1 says, *In the beginning was the Word, and the Word was with God, and the Word was God.* God is the Father, the Son, and the Holy Spirit, and all three are God. *The same was in the beginning with God. All things were made by him; and without him was not anything made that was made. In him was life; and the life was the light of men* (John 1:2–4). Note the verse *In him was life and the life was the light of men.* This reminds me of John 10:10. *The thief cometh not, but for to steal, and to kill, and to destroy: I am come that they might have life, and that they might have [it] more abundantly.*

In Him is life, and life is the light of men that they might have life and have it more abundantly. The Amplified Version of John 10:10 says, *The thief comes only in order to steal and to kill and destroy. I came that they may have and enjoy life and have it in abundance to the full until if overflows.* This means it is not just enough, but it is more than enough. *In the beginning was the Word and the Word was with God, and the Word was God, and the same was in the beginning with God. All things were made by him* (John 1:1–3). He has not changed His subject matter. He is talking about the word. He is talking about Jesus. He is talking about the Son. *In him, the Word is life and life was the light of men.*

I came that you might have life. You will never have abundant life outside of God's word. You will never have true life outside of God's word because the word came or was sent so that you might have life more abundantly. *And the light shineth in darkness; and the darkness comprehended it not* (John 1:5). The light (the word) shines in darkness. Before the light came, the mind (the thinker, chooser, feeler, understanding, reasoning, emotions) comprehended not, understood it not, and could not think like that.

> *There was a man sent from God, whose name was John. The same came for a witness, to bear witness of the Light, that all men through Him might believe. He was not that Light, but was sent to bear witness of that Light. That was the true Light, which lighteth every man that cometh into the world. He was in the world, and the world was made by him, and the world knew him not. He came unto his own, and his own received him not. But as many as received him, to them gave he power to become the sons of God, even to them that believe on his name.* (John 1:6–12)

I still believe the biggest difference in religion is Jesus. Everybody in some form of religion believes in a higher power or a god. Yet, when you start talking about Jesus is the Son of God that is when the problem begins. They fail to realize that this is our biggest benefit. It is not that Jesus is of God, but that Jesus is the Son of God. If you do not believe that Jesus is the Son of God, how could you ever believe that you could be the son or daughter of God?

That is where the difference starts. This is why we just cannot generalize God. When we generalize God, we lessen the importance of Jesus as Son. Afterward, we get into the religious rhetoric where you begin to compromise. At this point, there is no unity and there is no faith. There is no coming together unless you believe that Jesus is the Son of God. Anyone who does not believe in the Father and in the Son is anti-Christ (1 John 2:22).

That is where we differ. That is where the separation is made. That is why they are them and we are us. It does not matter about all the other stuff, but when people deny the place that Jesus holds, we have a problem. That is the only problem people have. They can believe in many things, but when it comes back to Jesus, now we have a problem. You cannot resolve the problem unless you know the Son. He is the path, the bridge, the way, and the truth.

> *But as many as received him, to them gave he power to become the sons of God, even to them that believe on his name: Which were born, not of blood, nor of the will of the flesh, nor of the will of man, but of God. And the Word was made flesh, and dwelt among us, (and we beheld his glory, the glory as of the only begotten of the Father,) full of grace and truth.* (John 1:12–14)

This is Jesus! When we were talking about the Father, Jesus did not come to speak, to do, and to show Himself. He came to speak, to do, and to show the Father. I explained that Jesus was only the expression of God's heart coming out of His mouth, out of God's mouth, out of the Father's mouth, and that is what *you* are. *And the word became flesh.* This means the Father spoke, flesh wrapped itself around the word, and now we beheld His glory. This is the same thing that He wants to happen in you. He wants the thing that He speaks over you to wrap itself around your flesh so that you and the word would become flesh.

You are only the expression of God's heart coming out of His mouth. Whatever He says, that is who you are. Whatever He says to do, that is what you can do. Whatever He has given us, this is what you have. *And the Word was made flesh, and dwelt among us, (and we beheld his glory, the glory as of the only begotten of the Father,) full of grace and truth* (John 1:14).

John is talking about how Jesus is the light. Proverbs 23:7 says, *For as he thinketh in his heart, so is he: Eat and drink, saith he to thee; but his heart is not with thee.* The thinker, the soul, the mind, the feeler, chooser, reasoning, emotions, and understanding is not lining up with what is in the heart. This is just like saying "I love you" out loud but you are really thinking that you hate that person's guts. So what was the real thing in your heart? Is it what you said or what you were thinking? As a man thinketh in his heart so is he. The scripture is eluding that a person is saying this or doing that, but his heart is far from it. People say they want to walk in the prosperity of God, but yet they do not want to work or get a job. The basis of this scripture is how a person is thinking, not what they are saying. Many of you have contrary thinking, going along with what you are saying. What you are saying is not making a difference in your life because you are not thinking in line with what you are saying.

Many of you know we have "gates" or entrances to our heart. We have the eye gate, the ear gate, and the mouth gate. The reason we need to understand this that more word will only make the old word better. If the old word is not good, it cannot get better. It is only good if it is working. If you are not doing what you already know, to get something new is not going to make it better.

Suppose I got a piece of something to do a certain task. Now, I have another piece that is going to make better what the first piece was designed to do. If I am not doing the first task, the second piece cannot make the first piece better. Unfortunately, this is what we have been doing in the body of Christ. We have the very word that we may know and understand. However, because we are not doing what we know, to get anything else is not going to make the word we have better. It will not get better until we start doing what we know that is good. I am not trying to give you something new. I am trying to make something that you already know work. I am trying to make it good, trying to get you to do it. I am trying to make your understanding of Jesus, being who He is in your life, better. I am trying to make it apply to your life so that you can see the results in your life. Then we can get to making it better.

You have got a lot of word in you; but in comparison to what you have in you, is your life good, or is it just okay? Jesus came to give you abundant life to the full until it overflows. Is it full and overflowing in your life? Ephesians 3:20 states, *Now unto him that is able to do exceeding abundantly above all that we ask or think.* Can you still think of something you do not have? If so, then there's something you can ask that you have not received.

The Abundance of the Heart

Proverbs 4:23 says, *Keep thy heart with all diligence; for out of it are the issues of life.* When the heart is full, the things that come forth out of your heart are your words. You can speak things, but until it is in your heart in the fullness, it is not going to create what you say. It is not going to manifest what you say if it is not from the fullness of your heart. You can speak out of pain, lack, or insufficiency. However, when you speak out of abundance, good, or bad, you will not delay but you will produce what you say. You are not going to have what you say just because you say what you say. You are going to have what you say when you say it in its fullness and in abundance.

Jesus is the way, the truth, and the light. Jesus is the path. Jesus is the bridge. Jesus is the door. *But the path of the just is as the shining light, that shineth more and more unto the perfect day* (Proverbs 4:18). Who is He talking about: the word or His Son? We established the light. This means the light brightens more and more toward that perfect day. What is the perfect day for you? When you get a new car? Waking up? The perfect day for me is when

Jesus returns. Everything else is gravy. Everything else is lacking. Everything else still needs to be adjusted and be corrected, but after that, it is all over.

This helps me to be patient when people make promises to do something. My favorite response to this is they have time until Jesus comes, so we are not even going to worry about it. Up until Jesus comes, you have time to do what you say you are going to do. After Jesus comes, you do not even need to worry about it.

The Word Is the Needful Thing

The way of the wicked is as darkness: they know not at what they stumble (Proverbs 4:19). Again the mind (the soul), is the thinker, the feeler, and the chooser. It is the reasoning, the emotion, and it is the understanding of the soul (mind). This is why the word is so important, because it helps us to walk in the spirit.

My son, attend to my words; incline thine ear unto my sayings (Proverbs 4:20). Here is the Son, the word, and Jesus while all at the same time He is talking about you.

Let them not depart from thine eyes; keep them in the midst of thine heart. For they are life unto those that find them, and health to all their flesh (Proverbs 4:21–22). The ear gate, mouth gate, and eye gate are the gates or entrances into our heart. Again, we are talking about the word. We are talking about allowing the word to manifest Himself in you. The word is the expression of God's heart coming out of His mouth and now we are being it. We have to think like that. We just cannot receive the word and say, "Oh that was nice. I wonder what that means?"

You have to become what and who He says you are, and not what your lack of understanding or this world's teaching of understanding has made you to be. *Keep thy heart with all diligence; for out of it are the issues of life* (Proverbs 4:23). Remember, we have gates to our heart: eye gate, ear gate, mouth gate. *Put away from thee a forward mouth, and perverse lips put far from thee. Let thine eyes look right on, and let thine eyelids look straight before thee. Ponder the path of thy feet, and let all thy ways be established"* (Proverbs 4:24-26).

If all of this (word) is not leading you to a place, then what place does all of this have? Jesus is not trying to be the destination for you. Jesus is not trying to get you to rest in Him. He is trying to show you, put a spotlight on, and give you a path to the Father. When you understand that, it will become clearer to what His place in your life should be, and how to give Him place in your life.

If I receive the word, yet I am not doing according to the word, then I am still going to be in the same place where I was before I got the word. If I get the word and do not allow the word to be effective in my life, then I have not changed. If I do not allow what He said to shine a light on whatever is dark, then whatever He said was not a light for me.

Turn not to the right hand nor to the left: remove thy foot from evil (Proverbs 4:27). I want you to get to the point that you realize that you have got this word that you received whenever you received it. It is supposed to be a light. It is supposed to be a path. It is supposed to lead you somewhere. It is supposed to make you better. It is supposed to become a part of who you are. Just think about a word you have heard. What has it done for you?

Until you really know His purpose, you will never benefit fully from what He has done. We know Jesus, and thank God for Jesus. However, are you fully benefiting from Jesus? Has knowing the word changed the way that you think? Has it changed the way you feel? Has it changed the things you choose? Has it made anything better in your life, or are you still the same before He came? Remember He has come to give abundant life.

Become the Word

James 1:17–18 says, *Every good gift and every perfect gift is from above, and cometh down from the Father of lights, with whom is no variableness, neither shadow of turning. Of his own will begat he us with the word of truth, that we should be a kind of firstfruits of his creatures.*

Just think about all that we have talked: the truth, the way, and the will. We should be a kind of firstfruits of His creatures.

> *Wherefore, my beloved brethren, let every man be swift to hear, slow to speak, slow to wrath: For the wrath of man worketh not the righteousness of God. Wherefore lay apart all filthiness and superfluity of naughtiness, and receive with meekness the engrafted word, which is able to save your souls.* (James 1:19–21)

The word not only has to be heard, but it has to be engrafted and become who you are. Remember, *and the word was made flesh* (John 1:14). It has to be a part of who you are. You just cannot hear it. You just cannot know it. You have to become it.

It is the engrafted word which is able to save your soul, your spirit, and your flesh. What is the word trying to change in you? It is your thinker, your feeler, your emotions, your chooser, your reasoning, and your understanding. This is what the word is trying to do. It is trying to get you to agree more with God and less on what you were brought up on and learned in the world and accustomed to.

But be ye doers of the word, and not hearers only, deceiving your own selves (James 1:22). It does not matter if you just heard it. It does not matter if you know it; if you are not doing it then it is not engrafted. *For if any be a hearer of the word, and not a doer, he is like unto a man beholding his natural face in a glass: For he beholdeth himself, and goeth his way, and straightway forgetteth what manner of man he was* (James 1:23–24). When you see the word, hear the word, and understand the word, it is supposed to *make* you the word. It is supposed to help you see who you are.

When you leave after hearing the word, you are not supposed to change that image. You come to church and you hear, "Be nice," then when you leave you should resemble what was given. In previous sermons, I have talked about love and how we are supposed to love. I have talked about how love is the DNA to signify that you belong to God, because God is love. If you want to be His child, there has to be love in you. Love is what flows through Him. This same love has to flow through you, also. I know it can be hard to love people when they do you wrong. However, that is what you are supposed to do.

You heard the word on love, you read the word on love; now, do not forget to do the word about love. Do not look at love and see it as God, and then go and not let love be you. That is what the word is for. It is for you to love. It is to create in you *as man thinketh in his heart.* How are you thinking? It is how you are being conformed, shaped, and made to be. If you are not thinking like God, you are not going to be like God, and you are not going to act like God. If you are not thinking like this, then you are not going to represent like this. Only when you are thinking like this (godly), then you will be like this.

It does not matter how long it takes. You did not come into this world as a fully grown child. You were a baby and then you grew into an adult. Growth in the word of God is the same way. You are not going to come into this way of living and do everything right, but it should be a progression. You should be getting better. It does not matter about wanting and getting and needing, and desiring new word when that old word you received has not made your life good. When you know you are not doing what you know, why would you want something else to know and to do but not do that as well?

> *But whoso looketh into the perfect law of liberty, and continueth therein, he being not a forgetful hearer, but a doer of the work, this man shall be blessed in his deed. If any man among you seem to be religious, and bridleth not his tongue, but deceiveth his own heart, this man's religion is vain.* (James 1:25–26)

When you understand and know something, yet you do not bridle your tongue to speak that which you know, then you cannot become what you know because you are not speaking what it is you know. What is the sense then in you saying that you believe if you have a religion, when what you believe and have a religion for does not work? Jesus came to give you life, and He came to give life more abundantly. So why is His abundance not manifested or evident in your life? How can you get and see the life more abundantly if you do not allow the word to be who you are?

As we go deeper into the aspect of our soul, having our mind being renewed by Jesus the word, we are going to see the importance of how we think. We will see the importance of what we should think, and how we think we should conform to His word. It is going to be vitally important. It may not have been important to you in your past, but I am hoping it will be important to you now.

Pure religion and undefiled before God and the Father is this, To visit the fatherless and widows in their affliction, and to keep himself unspotted from the world (James 1:27). In other words, do not allow the world to contaminate you. You can be in the midst of the world, but yet it does not affect you. You become the penicillin, the antidote, and the cure for the world and not the world becoming the sickness over you. What is greater: light or darkness? If we are to be that same light as Jesus was the light for us, or be the light for the world, then why are we being affected by the darkness? Why are we not allowing the light to affect the darkness?

My feeling has always been that I am not trying to deal with the darkness. I am trying to bring the light to the darkness. If I go into a dark room, I do not shoot the darkness out of the room. I turn on the light and the darkness flees. What you are trying to do is to get the darkness out of your life. I am saying do not worry about trying to get the darkness out of your life, just bring the light and the darkness *will* leave your life. If I am the light and I walk into a dark room, that room will be illuminated by the light in me. Basically, if I go into a place of confusion and because I have calmness in me, calmness should be in the place. It is not because of it, but because of me. This is when the word makes sense. This is when the word has effect: when you become the word, and not just you knowing the word.

The Word in Our Hearts

Now, how do we get things into our hearts? As you know, the gates to our hearts are the eyes, ears, and mouth. John 14:1 says, *Let not your heart be troubled.* How do you let trouble get to your heart? It is by what you see, what you hear, and what you say. We can cause our hearts not to be troubled by not speaking trouble, not looking at trouble, and not listening to trouble. I want that to be clear. *Let not your heart be troubled. Ye believeth in God believeth also in me.* What is Jesus saying? He is saying, "In the beginning was the word and the word was with God and the word was God." He said, "When you believe in God, you believe in me, because I was in Him at the beginning."

In my Father's house there are many mansions: if it were not so, I would have told you (John 14:2). Just briefly I wish to address one of the subjects we as believers have an issue about, which is a longing and desire to go to and have the experience of being in heaven. The sting and strength of death is the fear of death. When you quit fearing death, it will not have a stronghold on your mind. You fear death because you see it as a loss, but to live in God and die in God is really a gain. When we quit fearing our ultimate place in heaven, then there is nothing that the devil can do. Whether I am here or there, I am good in God. We will not long for heaven when we are not going to do our part down here on earth. When we do not long for that experience with the Father, then we are not going to do what Jesus tells us to do to get there. In order to have the experience with the Father in heaven, we must follow the instructions here. It is a road map to get there. There are detailed things to do so that we can find our way to Him. If we do not want to be with Him, we are not going to do what it takes to follow the instruction to get to Him.

Also, when the destination that the instruction is taking us to is not the emphasis, then we will put more emphasis on the instruction. Not being focused on where you are going can open the door for distractions. For example, if you are heading to Miami from Georgia in a car, and not in a plane, it is going to take you some time. The trip may not be as pleasant as it could be. You are taking a long trip in a car, and along the way, the devil is going to try to uproot and destroy you, making your life miserable. Yet when you know the benefit and the reward in getting to the destination, it is worth everything and every effort you go through to get there. So then you are not going to stop along the way or turn back and go home.

The emphasis should not be put on the journey. The emphasis is put on the destination so that the journey is worth traveling. If you do not put an emphasis on where you are going, you will never make the journey or follow the instructions He is telling you to get you there. It does not help you to look at what He is telling you to do if you don't follow the instructions. When you get to the end of the journey you will see the benefits of following the instructions. Jesus will not benefit you if you just look at, "He told me to love everybody." What is going to benefit you more than anything else is you looking at what the instructions will manifest and not what the instructions tell you to do.

Remember to keep your eyes focused on the end of the journey and not just the journey.

> *In my Father's house are many mansions: if it were not so, I would have told you. I go to prepare a place for you. And if I go and prepare a place for you, I will come again, and receive you unto myself; that where I am, there ye may be also.* (John 14:2–3)

I know we are ultimately talking about the return of Jesus and ultimately a place in heaven, but how many of you know that Jesus is still here right now in His word? You cannot separate Jesus the word from who He is. Jesus said He will come to you to take you where He is so that where He is, you can be there also. Yet you hear what He says, but you do not receive what He says to become what He says. How can you be what He is? How can you be in that place of total peace if you do not do what He did to be in peace or at peace? There is a road map, a path, and a journey He wants to take you on to a destination that He has prepared for you. *And whither I go ye know, and the way ye know* (John 14:4). How do you know? He is telling you.

For God, the issue, trouble, or the problem is never what you do not know to do. I thank God for mercy and grace. Mercy and grace covers my ignorance; however, there is no cover for my lack of willingness. He is not dealing with things you do not know. He says you know *this,* but you just do not do *this.* He says you know the way, but you just do not want to take the journey. You say, "But I do not know which way to go." Jesus replies, "Well, do not worry about it, just make this step." Then you make the excuse, "I still do not know," but in reality, you do know. Jesus told you to make a step. He told you to do this and that. He told you to be this and that. *That is* the way you know.

> *Thomas saith unto him, Lord, we know not whither thou goest; and how can we know the way? Jesus saith unto him, I am the way, the truth, and the life: no man cometh unto the Father, but by me.* (John 14:5–6)

Some of you may be saying, "Well, Lord, I do not know what I should do." Yes, you do. You know what He told you to do. You just do not think it is going to work. You simply do not believe it enough to do it so it can work out, but please do not say, "I do not know."

He is the way. He is the truth. He is the life. No man can come unto the Father but by Him. That means outside of Jesus you can never get to your destination. Without Him, you can never get to the Father. You cannot get to Holy of Holies. You cannot get to that "place," unless you come by way of Jesus. He is the path. *If ye had known me, ye should have known my Father also: and from henceforth ye know him, and have seen him* (John 14:7). How? It is because you have seen Jesus.

What effect does the way, the truth, the life have? We think that it affects only our spirit. It affects our spirit which in turn affects our soul. The way is what you choose, the truth is what you think, and the life is what you experience. Jesus is the way, the truth, and the life. I choose the way, I think the truth, and I experience the life. This occurs in my soul or the thinker, feeler, and chooser. What you feel (your emotions) is what you experience.

People allow what they experience to be based on what is going on instead of what they think, know, or choose. Your experiences for your life should be based on what is the way, or what is the truth. This is where the emotions that you have should come from. Emotions should never be based on circumstances and situations. They are based on your thinking. You can have the same identical situation to happen in your life and get two different emotions. It is not based on the situation. It is based on how you were thinking at that time. Since this is the case, I know you do not have to be subject to your emotions. Your emotions are subject to your thinking. This is what you will experience when you think right. *As a man thinketh in his heart* (Proverbs 23:7).

Now that you know you are not subject to situations and circumstances, what are you going to line your thinking up with? Is it what the world says or what God says? God said, "I am not talking about what you do not know." He said, "I am talking about what you do know." This is the life He came to give you. He said you are the head and not the tail, only above and never again beneath. This is what you should experience. It is because that is what you should think. You have chosen that way, you think that truth, and now you should experience that life. That is the way, the truth, and the life. I choose the way, I think the truth, and I live and experience the life. You are not the sick, but you are the healed protecting your health. That is the way, that is the truth, and that is the life. Choose the way, think the truth, and experience the life. He said, "If I be for you, who can be against you?" That is the way, that is the truth, and that is the life. Choose the way, think the truth, and experience the life.

What else do you know? What other word do you know? What else has He said about you? I am not trying to give you something else to choose. I am not telling you to think of something else. I am saying, "What have you known Him to have said to you?" This is His way, His truth, and His life. This is why Jesus was sent.

If you want to maximize the fullness of Jesus' potential in your life, then choose His way, think His truth, and experience His life. Why would you want to think on what somebody else said? They are not God. They did not come to give you life more abundantly. So why are you putting more value in that? Why would you want to accept what somebody else does for you? I am not telling you what to think. I am telling you to know what to think.

You have to choose the way and think the truth. *Yea, let God be true, but every man a liar* (Romans 3:4). That is why He said study to show yourself approved (2 Timothy 2:15). I am not trying to tell you what God said to you. I am saying whatever God said to you that it is His way, His truth, and His life. Now you choose it, you think it, and you experience it. Experience it as that emotion; it is that feeling. When I experience that, it is going to make me happy. You are trying to experience what He said when you have not chosen it. You are trying to experience what He said when you are not thinking it.

That is His way, which is His truth, and that is His life for you. He said no weapon formed against you shall prosper (Isaiah 54:17). No weapon, regardless of how it is formed or where it is formed against you, shall prosper, and every tongue that rises up shall be condemned. That is His way, that is His truth, and that is His life that He came to give you. Do not settle for anything less. I am not saying the journey will not be difficult. I am not saying that the devil will not try to stop you, but I am saying let the end be better than the journey. If what I am expecting is better than what I am experiencing now, then I will go through what I am experiencing to get what I am expecting. I have not arrived there; this is just a journey to get there. I am not going to stop on the journey until I get to the destination.

Jesus is the door, the bridge, the path, and He is life. Let Him take you to the destination. Will you do it? We are in this together. It is not enough for me to understand this and start walking in it. We all must come to the knowledge of the Son of God. When you start reading the word of God, you will start to find your place and purpose in your life. You are going to understand that this is the path, this is the way, this is the truth, this is the life, this is the step, and this is the journey. You can say to yourself that this is where He has taken me to so that I can get to where I am supposed to be. This is how I am supposed to be—transformed into the very image of God. This is what I am supposed to be like. This is my reflection.

I know what is going on; every word that God has spoken to you is coming alive. You said, "I put that word on the shelf, and I did not allow that to be the way." "I put that word on the shelf, and I did not allow it to be the truth." "I put that word on the shelf, and I did not allow that to be the life." Now that you know better you can decide to let His word lead you. You are going to let that be a part of you. You are going to take that word and let that become you. *And the word became flesh* (John 1:14). You are the very expression of God's love and heart toward you. That is who you are. You are what He says you are. You have what He says you can have. What He says you can do, that is what you do. It is because His heart is speaking His desire for your life. His word is in you: that is what you are.

CHAPTER 3

Renewing the Mind

We make the things of God and our lives as Christians too complicated. Is that really what we want? Do we really just want Him? If people can be affected, disappointed, or mad at Him because of a circumstance, situation, or event, or because of what they are not or did not get, is it really Him that they are seeking?

Are you seeking the things He has, or what you think He can give you? You can never seek the things above Him. He will never release the things in your life when it takes the place of Him. You must get to the point that all your desires, the thing that makes you the happiest, which gives you the most joy and fulfills you the greatest are not circumstances or situations, people, and events. It is not about what you get or what you do not get. It is not what happens or does not happen.

It is all about Him and the relationship you have with Him. "I just want you," has to be your testimony. It has to be the voice of your heart that comes out of your mouth, for out of the abundance of the heart, the mouth speaks (Matthew 12:34). What is the abundance of your heart? Is it worry, doubt, fret, things, or issues, or is it the love for Him? If it is the love for Him, then that is what should be coming out of your mouth. "I just want you." Your life is good all the time, because He is the same today and forever more.

I hope *Developing the Complete You* has convinced you that everything is established on our intimate, personal relationship with God. Just to recap, in previous chapters our spirit man, who is the real part of us, is developed by our intimate, personal relationship with the Father God. There is no substitute, and our spirits cannot be established any other way. Nobody else can go to the Father for you. Some people think they can; however, we do not have priests who can go to the Father for us. No one can get saved, delivered, or healed for you. It does not matter how anointed, appointed, or called that person is. You can desire to have the things of God in your life, but if you do not want to cultivate an intimate, personal relationship with the Father, then you are not getting what is in His hand.

In chapter 2, we learned that our soul (our thinker, our chooser, and our feeler) is developed by our relationship with Jesus the Son, who is the word, which can affect how we think and decide. Later we will prove that our bodies, the flesh, and the things we do are affected by the Spirit of God. He will pour out His Spirit on all our flesh (Acts 2:17). It is the supernatural ability on the natural flesh that gives us the ability to do things that we could not do before He came upon us. It is the anointing of God upon us that makes things possible.

Now that you understand the importance of God the Father, God the Son, and what part of you these two parts develop, how do you obtain the growth? Development occurs when we renew our minds. You cannot desire the anointing until your mind is renewed. If you get the anointing without your mind being renewed, you may do what "you" want and not what "He" wants. You cannot get your mind renewed until you get a relationship. You are not going to know what He wants without a relationship.

We have made it so complicated until it is very hard for us to live this life as a Christian. It should not be hard. Now, we are going to make it simple and so easy that you can do it. You just have to choose to.

When it comes to renewing the mind, we are still talking about, primarily, the Son Jesus developing our mind, our soul, or the intellect part of us.

Romans 12:1 says, *I beseech you therefore, brethren, by the mercies of God, that ye present your bodies a living sacrifice, holy, acceptable unto God, which is your reasonable service.* If you do not present your body, nobody is going to present it for you. If you do not bring it to the altar, your body is not coming on its own, unless you are dead and we roll you down in a casket. However, that is not what He wants. At that point, it is too late. You cannot make any decision in the casket.

Your decision has to be made while you are still living here on the earth. You must present your body a living, breathing, and active sacrifice. Anything living ought to be doing something. Anything dead ought to be buried. Your body should be living, active, and motivated, not just sitting on your seat and doing nothing. Your body should not be on the sideline, while the game is going on. It should be a part of it as an active participant in the game. Furthermore, it should not be just participating, but adding value and supply to the game and bringing strength to it.

One of the things that I share with people all the time is that in several ways, I can tell whether or not you are an effective member of a church. First, if you are not there, nobody misses you. You are not being missed because you are not doing anything. Second, if you are doing something and somebody who just got there can do what you do, then you may not be doing that much, especially if you can be replaced very quickly. Do not be on the sidelines, but be actively participating.

Sacrifice

Most Christians, traditionally like to bring sacrifices to God. We sing songs like "We Bring the Sacrifice of Praise," and that is fine as a starting place, but you should not have a life of sacrifice. Sacrifice means you give up something to do what you desire. In the olden days, they had to do a series of sacrifices just to stay clean; however, today, God is only asking for one. Jesus was our sacrifice. He was the sacrificial lamb. When He died on the cross, do you think somebody else needs to get on the cross to die again for us? Was it sufficient for all? His sacrifice was sufficient for us. Therefore, we should not have to make as many "sacrifices" as we are making.

For some of you, just to come to church is a sacrifice. For you to get involved in the church is a sacrifice because you are probably thinking about what you might have to give up. Giving in the offering is a sacrifice, because you think about what you were going to do with the money before you give it. However, the word says for us to be a *living sacrifice.* He is only asking for one sacrifice: our lives.

We make a series of sacrifices. It is all right to start off with a sacrifice, but once you give Him your life, everything else should become your reasonable service. He owns everything. So far you have given Him bits and pieces of yourself, instead of giving Him all of you. You want to give Him this part today, and it is a sacrifice. You want to give Him that part tomorrow, which is a sacrifice too. Yet if you give Him your life today, everything else becomes your reasonable service, because He owns all of you. It is not what you want, but it is what He wants. It is not what you want to do, but it is what He tells you to do. We must get to that holy place that says anything holy belongs to God: holy tithes, the holy temple, and be ye holy. You are holy!

The scripture tells us *unto God which is your reasonable service.* Again, when you give Him your life, everything else becomes a reasonable service. When you give Him your life, you do not have to make a series of sacrifices. You only have to make that one and ultimate sacrifice, which is to give Him all of you.

And be not conformed to this world: but be ye transformed. How are we going to be transformed? It is by the renewing of our minds now. You are not going to know what to be, how to think, or how to respond until you change how you think. *And be not conformed to this world: but be ye transformed by the renewing of your mind, that ye may prove what is that good, and acceptable, and perfect, will of God* (Romans 12:2).

Now, ask yourself this question, "Can God build His church on you?" Matthew 16:13 says, *When Jesus came into the coasts of Caesarea Philippi, he asked his disciples, saying, Whom do men say that I the Son of man am?* This is a good question.

> And they said, Some say that thou art John the Baptist: some, Elias; and others, Jeremias, or one of the prophets. He saith unto them, But whom say ye that I am? And Simon Peter answered and said, Thou art the Christ, the Son of the living God. And Jesus answered and said unto him, Blessed art thou, Simon Barjona: for flesh and blood hath not revealed it unto thee, but my Father which is in heaven. (Matthew 16:14–17)

Who revealed it to Simon Peter? Was it man? Was it Jesus? It was the Father. Jesus went on to say, *And I say also unto thee, That thou art Peter, and upon this rock I will build my church; and the gates of hell shall not prevail against it* (Matthew 16:18).

We understand that Peter received revealed or revelation knowledge. It was not just revelation knowledge itself, but the revelation knowledge in which Jesus is going to build His church on. He is going to build His church on the knowledge that Jesus is the Son of God and the anointed one. *Thou art the Christ, the anointed one and the Son of the Living God.* This is what Jesus wants to build His church on. If you do not identify and recognize who He is, you will never become who you are supposed to be. We are to be conformed and changed into the very image of Jesus, who came to be the example for who we are to be. Remember, in the book of Romans, we are being transformed by the renewing of our mind.

You do not know how you are supposed to be because you were not in the garden of Eden where it all began. All you know is what this sinful world says who you ought to be, but this is not nearly what we are supposed to be. Jesus came to be an example of what we are supposed to be like without man's sin. If you do not know that, you cannot receive that, and you will never become that. God will give you the keys, and the gates of hell will not prevail against it!

The gates of hell should not be your door. The gates of hell should be of those who have not come to the knowledge and the understanding of who Jesus is and have not accepted Him as their Lord and savior. The "gates of hell" is not your house. It is not your thing. When you know who He is and who you are, the attention is not on you. It is on those that do not know Him yet. That is what should not prevail. We should be on the offense.

If we are the light, we should not be just standing in the light. We should be the light in the midst of the darkness. If we are the example, we should not be just the example for one another. We should be the example for those who do not know Him at all. We should not talk to one another and be the light for one another. We should not tell one another what we are supposed to be doing, but instead find those that do not know anything and tell them. Christians like to preach to one another, but you cannot tell someone else what to do when you do not even know yourself.

It works just the opposite if you are trying to grow. If you are speaking to people who are on the same level as you, they cannot tell you something more than what you already know. You should seek people who are above you because they have the blueprint from their experience. They are the ones that could tell you how to get there, to the place where you want to be. Since they know more they will be more effective, because they have already been where you want to go. What many people should do is speak to people below them because they are the ones that should be open to listen. They are the ones that need to get to where you are. That is the place for them to learn and grow, but not for your growth. Please stop talking to folks on your level about your problems. They cannot give you the answer. If they had the answer, they would not have the same problem.

I reiterate, the gates of hell should not be your door. The gates of hell should not be your house. The gates of hell should be those that you are witnessing to and those that you have been the light for. Remember, Romans 12:2 says, *And be not conformed to this world.* The word *conform* means to act in accordance to or be one with the world; do not become similar in form with the world. This means that we do not conform to this world, act in accordance to, become one with, or become similar in form with this world. When the world acts and responds one way, you should not become similar in form or one with them in their actions.

If there is no difference between Christians and people of the world, then what is the difference? If you are acting just like them, what makes them want to act like us? 2 Corinthian 6:14 says, *Be ye not unequally yoked together with unbelievers: for what fellowship hath righteousness with unrighteousness? and what communion hath light with darkness?*

The Amplified Version states, *Do not be unequally yoked with unbelievers. Do not make mismanaged alliance with them or come under a different yoke with them inconsistent with your faith.* In other words, do not get in line with them or do things inconsistent with what you say you believe, or what you are living, standing and believing God for. *For what fellowship hath righteousness with unrighteousness? and what communion hath light with darkness?"* *And what concord hath Christ with Belial? or what part hath he that believeth with an infidel?* (2 Corinthians 6:14). What concord or acting in accordance has Christ with Belial? What agreement does Christ have with the devil?

> *And what agreement hath the temple of God with idols? for ye are the temple of the living God; as God hath said, I will dwell in them, and walk in them; and I will be their God, and they shall be my*

people. Wherefore come out from among them, and
be ye separate, saith the Lord, and touch not the
unclean thing; and I will receive you. (2 Corinthians
6:16–17)

Do not conform to this world. Do not act similar to this world.
If you are doing so, you are no better than the world. You have to
come out from among them. If you are the only saved person on
your job, does everybody know it? Do you just "blend in" until
they cannot tell the difference? Is your "standing" different from
their "standing," if their standing is not God? Are your actions
different from their actions if their action is not of God? Are you
a conformist? You cannot be like the world. You cannot think like
the world. You cannot act like the world. You cannot be one with
the world, but be transformed to God. *And be not conformed to this*
world but be ye transformed. The word *transformed* means to change
the appearance, change the form, or change the condition of. It
means to be converted.

Since you have been born-again, what has transformed in you?
Has your appearance changed, or are you still looking like you were
before you got saved? Has your form changed, or are you still acting
like you were before you got saved? Has your condition changed,
or are you still living like you were before you got saved? Have you
truly been converted? If nothing has changed, what was the benefit
of you getting saved? If you are still looking the same, talking the
same, acting the same, and living the same, then what has changed?

Again, how are we going to be transformed? The Bible states
by the renewing of our minds. *Renew* means to restore, resume, or
return to the original state. Now, if you do not know what your
original state was, you cannot return back to it. Jesus came to
be the example of the original state of man. He came to be the
example of what we are to be like so that we do not have to be like
this world.

If so be that ye have heard him, and have been
taught by him, as the truth is in Jesus: That ye put

> *off concerning the former conversation the old man,*
> *which is corrupt according to the deceitful lusts.*
> (Ephesians 4:21–22)

The only thing many of you may know is what the world has told you, and that information is corrupt. The world's standard is corrupt. Its political ways are corrupt. You have to put those things off and take on the nature of Jesus and the things that will take you to Jesus. We are talking about renewing our minds. If we do not do this, we will react, respond, and speak just like the world has taught us to.

And that ye put on the new man, which after God is created in righteousness and true holiness (Ephesians 4:24). You must start thinking and acting in a new way. This is the new man He wants you to put on. This means you cannot "cuss" out anybody that does you wrong. That is the old man, and you have to put him off and put on this good man, which is the new man.

You have to do good to those that treat you badly. I know it seems hard, but that is what God requires. Everything in life was probably difficult when you first started. Walking was hard when you first started. Talking was hard when you first start it, (sometimes it is still difficult). Driving a car, riding a bicycle, or even swimming was hard. Anything is hard when you first started, but if you do it long enough, it becomes a part of who you are.

Nobody said things were always going to be easy the first time you do it. Just because it is hard the first time you try something new does not mean you stop it at the first time. If you do, you will never renew your mind, and never get it back to what it is supposed to be like. Consistency is the key to the breakthrough. It is not you try it one time, and no, it does not work. You have not worked the process long enough for it to work.

By the renewing of your mind, "you" must first begin to do so. The relationship that you desire to develop with the Father will make the benefit of Jesus greater in your life. It will put Him in the proper place that He was sent to be in your life.

Now please understand this, you will never greatly benefit from Him living the life of obedience; by Him taking the "stripes upon His back" for your healing; and from Him shedding His untainted, unblemished blood. You will not benefit from all that He did if you do not understand why He was sent and the purpose for which He was given to us. We will look at Him and say, "That's Him. That's not me." Or, you may go from one extreme to the other and say, "That's Him and I'm Him too," but the Bible never said that.

No, He did not say that Jesus is the only Son of God. He is the firstborn of many brethren. Your brother is not you, even though you both are sons of the same mother. You have the same rights and privileges that come with being in the family, but you may not do the same thing because you were not sent for the same purpose. He did not come to tell you what to do. He came to do what He was sent for. He is trying to tell you how He thought so that you can think like He thinks; not so you can do what He did, but so that you can do what God tells you to do.

By the renewing of your mind, that ye may prove what is that good, and acceptable, and perfect, will of God (Romans 12:2). The word *proves* means to verify, test, and establish the truth. You have to prove God's word in your life. The word *good* means unspoiled, valid, healthy, sound, worthy, and happy; it also means a favorable quality, proper, genuine, and pleasant. So what is good about you? What is unspoiled, valid, healthy, and sound? Is your marriage sound? Is your life healthy? What is worthy, happy, and of a favorable quality? What is proper and genuine? Are you leather or are you pleather? What is the real deal about you?

People see a life that you present when you come to church, but will that be the same genuine life you have if we were to follow you home? Perhaps it is just the pleather that is presented, because you do not have any real leather? You are pretending that you have it, but you do not have the real deal, the *genuine* and the *pleasant*. I talked earlier about how more word or new word is only to make the old word better. It cannot be better until it is good. So what is the *good*?

It is only good if it is being used. If it is not good, it cannot be better, and it is not going to be good until you are doing it. If it is real, then it is good. If it is good, then He will give you some word that will make it better. He is not going to give you anything else to make it better when you have not yet made what you have good and genuine. If it is good, then it should be real and evident in your life that the goodness of God is there.

That ye may prove what is that good, and acceptable will of God. Acceptable means to take or receive and to consent or agree to. We cannot go to God and just pray for "things" unless what we are praying for has already been confirmed in the knowledge of our understanding that this is what He wants. If you are not sure if something is what God wants in your life, do not pray for it.

God is never going to give you something that you do not know is His will. Even if it is His will and you do not know it, it will not benefit you. You will not do what He wants you to do unless you have the knowledge of His purpose. Your prayer should be, "God, let your will be done. God, whatever You want to happen, let it happen. Whatever You have predestined to take place, let it take place." This will give you the life that God came to give you. It will not happen when you start trying to direct or govern what God ought to do. God already knows what He ought to do. He is trying to get you to line up with His will.

God is able to do exceedingly, abundantly, above all that you can ask or think. So why are you still asking? If He can do "more" than you can ask or think, why are you still asking for what you want, since He wants to bring you more than that? You should tell God to bring you what He wants for you. At this point, it will not be what "you" can ask, but it will be more than that. God will bring you something that you have no knowledge and understanding of ever receiving. The benefit is that He will bring it with the understanding of what you are to do with it.

Remember, as it was explained before, Jesus is the word, and the word was God, and the word was made flesh. The word and Jesus are the same. The biggest mistake that we make in the body of Christ is that we try to live by the Bible, and this is totally what we are to live by. The Bible is to lead us to the Father. The Father tells us what to live or how to live and what He tells us will line up with the Bible.

Let this walk be the example to lead you to Jesus. Jesus is the way, the bridge, and the door. Jesus is trying to direct you to the Father. Jesus is the Father's word, who revealed Himself to Peter. It was not what Jesus said, but it was what the Father revealed to Peter. It is not what you read in the Bible, but it is what the Father reveals. This is to get you to Him (the Father) and to reveal to you the life you are destined to live. The word is to lead you to Him, and then to His works. The works will always line up with what Jesus did, because Jesus is the example.

The Bible is what you should read all the time. It will tell you "how" to do certain things. It will not tell you "what" Jesus did all the time. Remember, when I said that Jesus spit in the ground, made some mud, and applied it on the eyes of the blind person and their eyes were opened? Now, that is what the Father told Jesus to do. So could you do what Jesus did: spit on the ground, make some mud, and go apply it on the eyes of a blind person, and will his eyes be opened to see?

No! What Jesus did and what God says was not to tell you "what to do." It was to show you that if you obey like Jesus did, then God will tell "you" what to do, and then it will work. Jesus did not want to come and be the person to say "do this, do this, do this, and do this." If He did, then you will be like a walking robot and that would never develop the relationship. If it were like that you will never go and hear what He has to say, or what He wants you to do. You will never let Him lead you and guide you.

Not that we are sufficient of ourselves to think any thing as of ourselves; but our sufficiency is of God; Who also hath made us able ministers of the new testament; not of the letter, but of the spirit: for the letter killeth, but the spirit giveth life. (2 Corinthians 3:5)

71

This is what the Pharisees and Sadducees tried to do, but they put people in bondage. They did not give them the liberty to know God for themselves. He wants to tell you what life you ought to have. Not in the "letter" or written word only. The letter is to tell you how to think and how to get to the Father, but who can tell you the life you ought to live?

Where are you going to find in the written word to whom to specifically talk to about a situation? Where are you going to find in the word the right business venture to invest into so that you can get a big return? I am talking about specifics, not just general. Where are you going to find in the word what to do about a specific situation toward a person that just cursed you out?

I know you are supposed to do well, but just doing *any* good is not always it. Now, slapping may feel good, but that is not the good He is telling you to do. Your *good* is not to the degree of what He wants. Remember, we talked about that *good and acceptable, perfect will of God*? You cannot determine what is good by what you want to do. You need to say, "God, what do you want me to do?" and *that* is good.

For example, you know God said to give someone a $100, but they gave them $10. Yet you say that is good enough. Wrong. It is not good enough when God told you to give them $100. See, you cannot get that in the word. You cannot get a "give a $100," in the written word. There is nowhere in the Bible where you can search and find where God said to give a specific person a $100 because they need it to convince him that you are a person of God.

Yet this Bible is what you want to live. You do not see the fullness of the manifestation of what God wants to do in your life because the Bible is not *all* the life. Your life will line up with the Bible. It should always line up with the Bible. However, it is not the total life He wants to give you. He wants to speak the word to you just like He spoke in revelation to Peter, "and upon this rock" (Matthew 16:18). What rock?

The rock is whatever He says. It is about whatever situation you need. You cannot find the specifics in this Bible, but it will lead you to Him, who has the specifics.

You cannot get your life just out of the Bible; you can only get your examples on how to live life. You can also get how you are to think. You can get how you are to respond. You can even get the attitude and the emotions you should carry, but you cannot get the specific act and work that you should do just from the Bible alone.

I am not talking about just always, because when you were first born again you needed the written word to follow. When you are a baby, you had certain limitations to your freedom. There were restrictions and more direct, precise instructions for those who were learning how to live according to God's kingdom. All of these instructions are only to get you to a point and a knowing of being able to choose and make decisions on your own. Every act of obedience is not just for that act of obedience that you do and perform. It is to empower you; it is to get you to a place where you will be ready for the ultimate act of obedience.

In other words, when Jesus made the decision to get on the cross, it did not happen instantly. Every act of obedience, up until that time, prepared Him for that final and only act, which was the most difficult one He faced—death!

If Jesus would not have obeyed God all of those other times, He would not have been prepared for the cross. This is the same way with you. This little act of obedience that God is telling you to do is not just for this one thing. It is to get you to a place of obeying Him all the time. It does not matter whether or not you do it for other things to happen. However, it does matter in your development when you obey God. If you do not do what God tells you to do, He will find someone else to get it done. It will not make your life better.

As the scripture says, you have to prove *what is that good, and acceptable, and perfect, will of God* (Romans 12:2). Your act of obedience will prove whether God's will is true or not. You will never know if something is the will and purpose of God, or you will not know His plan for your life if you are not willing to do it. If you are not willing to do it and prove it, He cannot go any further with you.

God knows that this proof is going to be necessary for you to walk in whatever you decide to do. It does not make any sense in walking, if you do not have an understanding of His will and if you are not secure in it. Otherwise, you will not be ready for it.

The portion of scripture we are meditating on right now is *that good, and acceptable, and perfect, will of God.* The word *perfect* means flawless, exact, absolute, pure, and complete. Excellence is the walk, but perfection is the destination. You never reach perfection here on earth. I know you think you can be perfect, but you are not. He wants you to strive for perfection. He wants you to reach and walk toward perfection, but you can walk in excellence along the way. Excellence is excelling in all that you are doing. Excellence means getting better as you go. I am being developed while I go, because when I get to that place of perfection, I will be complete.

You will never get to completion until He returns. God said that in a moment and in a twinkling of an eye, we should all be changed (1 Corinthians 15:52). If you were already perfect, there is no need for you to change. You would have already been changed. Change will be the final piece of the puzzle until your perfection has been completed. Until then, He will forever be perfecting you. Therefore, the pursuit of excellence is the walk.

Did you know you can produce excellence? If you are better today than you were yesterday at what you are doing, then that is excellence. If you are going to do better next week than what you are doing this week, that is excellence. You cannot be getting worse. This is how you judge in which direction you are going. Can you look at your past and see that you are doing more for God than you are now? Are you going up, or are you going down? Are you getting better, or are you getting worse? If at any other time in your life you were better in doing things for God, or walking for God, than you are now, then what direction did you go? You are going in a wrong direction. If you are going in the way of God then you will see increase, because He is a God that always increases. The sign of God's hands being on anything is indicated by increase being there. Nothing stays the same that God touches. Nothing! Nothing stays the same that God is involved in. If God is involved in it, it is getting better.

The will of God is a conscience choice. It is a control, a determination, and a desire. You just cannot accidentally fall into His will. It is a conscience choice that you decide to do. You must choose the way, think the truth, and experience the life.

This is a journey you are taking, which may be a lifetime of development. Remember, you have to prove God's word. Whatever He speaks to you, do it, regardless of the situation. Instead of speaking to God, a lot of people go and talk to another person, and they tell them what they think you ought to do. For example, if you were having marital problems, a person might advise you like this: "If I were you, I would leave him (or her)." They can even give you a scripture from the Bible to back up what they said. However, will that be what you ought to do if you had gone to God and found out what He wanted you to do?

It is the same thing with Jesus. Are you going to find what He did without going to God and find out what He wants? When you find out what God wants, it will always line up with what He said and did. He may not tell you exactly what Jesus did. Remember, the emphasis was not on the specific act, like Jesus spitting on the ground, making mud, and applying it on the eyes. The emphasis was getting the result.

You doing what Jesus did might not get the result, but you doing what God said will. So is proving God's word specifically doing what Jesus said, because were Jesus' words and actions His own? No. He only did what the *Father told Him to do*. So likewise, Jesus only wants you to do what the Father tells you to do. For example, if the Father tells Jesus to go left and for you to go right, I want you to go right and not left. Even if God tells me to spit on the ground and tells you to spit in the air, I want you to spit in the air and not on the ground. You see the difference? That is why the relationship with God the Father is vital.

Philippians 2:5 says, *Let this mind be in you, which was also in Christ Jesus.* The Bible is only to take you to the "mind-set" of Jesus and how He governs His life, but it is not just so that you can live.

If that perspective is correct, then everything He did you are going to have to do. You are going to have to walk on the water, feed a multitude of five thousand people with a two-piece fish dinner, and go to the cross. He does not want you to do what He did. Jesus said, *The works that I do shall he do also; and greater works than these shall he do.* Now, the works He did was not so much as "what" He did, but it was the obedience to the Father and what the Father told Him to do.

Now, in relation to Jesus, there will be similar things that we have in common. There are some things that all of us are supposed to have, such as two legs and two hands. Some of us have more hair than others. However, we are not all looking alike, and we have not all been called to do the same thing, even though what we do is connected by one purpose, one God, and one vision.

Yet there are some things that will contrast. Since Jesus is the head, He does not want you to be the head. He does not need another head, but He does need an arm, a leg, a hand, and a finger. Proverbs 23:7 says, *For as he thinketh in his heart, so is he.* When you read the word of God, let the mind-set that Jesus walks in also be in you. Jesus is our primary perfect example. He wants us to understand what Moses, Abraham, and David did: the right and the wrong, but not so we can necessarily do what they did. It is so we can think and understand what causes things to happen, and so we can understand our Father's way. It is not so that we can do what they did, but that we can identify when He is talking to us.

As you think in your heart, so are you. How so? Well, how are you thinking? Is it half-full or half-empty thinking? Are you more than able, or are you just doing half enough? Is it an opportunity or an obstacle? Is it a stepping stone or a stumbling block? Is it to develop you or to tear you down? How are you thinking? *Let this mind be in you.*

Let me illustrate this point with a more personal example. Here is something Pastor Creflo Dollar and I said for about five years straight during football season when we were in school together. Every football game, we started off saying this, even though we were not the most talented football squad there was. We had, maybe, twenty-five players on our team, and anybody that was any good played offense and defense. We did not know about playing one side of the ball, but we said that "as a man thinketh in his heart, so is he." This is what we used to say before every game.

The Man Who Thinks He Can

Walter D. Wintle

If you think you are beaten, you are;
If you think you dare not, you don't.
If you'd like to win, but think you can't
It's almost a cinch you won't.

If you think you'll lose, you've lost,
For out in the world we find
Success being with a fellow's will;
It's all in the state of mind...

We used to say these words before every game, and when we came out of that locker room, you could not tell us we were going to lose.

What mind frame do you carry? Do you carry a defeated mind-set or a victorious mind-set? Do you think of yourself as those who are subject to this world or as those that are conquerors of this world? How do you perceive yourself? Is your mind built upon the rock of knowledge that you have received from God?

When God says you are the head and not the tail; when He says you are above only and never again beneath; when He says that He has not given you the spirit of fear, but of love, power, and a sound mind; when He says that you do not have to accept and be subject to sickness, pain, and death, how do you think? Remember, *as a man thinketh in his heart, so is he.*

You can never see the benefit of what Jesus did if you do not think like Jesus thought. You will think that you are still subject to sickness and disease if you do not understand how He thought. You will think that you still have to die if you do not think like

Jesus thought. You will think that you have to walk in poverty, have nothing, and be in lack if you do not think like Jesus thought. You can never see the full benefit of Him being an example if you do not take the mind-set that He took. His mind-set was that "no weapon formed against me shall prosper." His mind-set was that "every tongue that rises up against me, I shall condemn." His mind-set was that "this is not more than I can bear." His mind-set was that "I have all strength and all sufficiency for all things. I can do all things through Christ."

I ask you again, how do you think? Do you think that your marriage is successful and the devil will not steal it? Do you think that you are happy? How do you think? Do you think it is hopeless, and it is not going to work? Well, if that is how you think, then you know what? It is not going to work. If you say, "I will never get a good job." You know what? You are right, you will not! How about say something like, "Nobody will ever give me a break." You know what? They will not. Here is another one, "I'm always going to live this defeated life." You know what? You will until you change how you think, because as a man thinketh in his heart, so is he.

Think big and your deeds will grow. Think small and you will fall behind. Think that you can and you will. It is all in the state of mind. Life's battles do not always go to the strongest or fastest man. Sooner or later, the man that wins is the fellow that thinks he can, and the one who thinks "I can do all things." I want you to have this state of mind. Will you do it?

Hear and Understand. See and Believe.

And Jesus said, "If you do not believe me for what I say, then believe me for what I do" (John 8:46; John 10:38). The things people hear they understand, but what they see they believe. You cannot convince people of what God can do in others, if you are not allowing God to do it in you. You cannot go to the world and say, "He is the light for you," if He is not the light in you. You cannot tell them that He can deliver them from their situation if He is not delivering you from your situation. You cannot tell them that He can heal them of every sickness and disease if you are still subject to it.

You see, you cannot walk in His will like that if you do not think like this. You cannot think like that until you have a relationship like that. So now in the next chapter we are going to talk about proving the word.

Chapter 4

Proving the Word

Before we move on to the next point which is proving God's word, I just want to keep fresh in your mind the points that we have already established.

Developing the Complete You is about relationship. It is about how our spirit is developed by an intimate, personal, one-on-one relationship with the Father. We cannot substitute anything for that relationship because everything that He is doing is to bring us back to that koinonia (communion) relationship with Him.

The next point we established is that Jesus the word is to renew our mind. Philippians 4:8 tells us to *think on these things*. Jesus is not the substitute for the Father. He is the bridge, the door, the way, and the path to get you to the Father. If you just stop with Jesus, you will minimize the effect and the things that Jesus came to do. Jesus came to lead you to the Father, not for you to think he is to be above the Father. It is to change how you think so that you can receive the Almighty Father in your life. Jesus was the Son of God and this is good. Since He was God's Son, then we can also be God's sons and daughters.

The final part we are working toward is God's Spirit upon the flesh which will give you supernatural abilities to do what you could not do before He came. That is the result; that is the work, which is manifestation. It is when you are starting in the trueness of who He is and not just the words of what He said. We can speak who God is, but very few Christians are showing it. Proving the word is how we can show God's will to ourselves and others.

We left off with our understanding in chapter 3 that Jesus is the word. Romans 12:2 says, *And be not conformed to this world: but be ye transformed by the renewing of your mind, that ye may prove.* Renewing of the mind means restoring back to its original state. The word *proves* means to verify, test, or to establish the truth. The word of God is only an assumption until it has been proven, and it is only proven in the midst of a test. You can say whatever you want to, but until you pass the test, it is not real, it is not settled, and it is not verified. The truth has not been established in your life.

Jesus said, *I am the way, the truth and the life.* You choose the way, you think the truth, and you experience the life. This is what you have to do. It is not over until you experience all that He says you can have. 2 Timothy 2:15 says, *Study to shew thyself approved unto God, a workman that needeth not to be ashamed, rightly dividing the word of truth.* This is what you must do: establish the truth by verifying, testing, and studying to show thyself approved. It does not matter what somebody *else* has established to be the truth, or who else other than yourself has been established to be verified to do works in God.

We limit God: not by God's ability, but by our thinking. God can do it, He wants to do it, and He will do it eventually. Yet, He will not ever do it until we start changing the way we think and perceive. That is what is limiting Him.

Proving God's word is our objective, but you have to study to show yourself approved. It is not based on somebody else's study that is going to establish you. It is not based on what somebody else is doing, how they are living, or what they have verified that is going to establish you. That is an individual walk—your own personal choice and decision. One revelation that you will need to receive is that if God is going to hold you accountable for your life, He is going to put your life in your authority and under your power.

God is never going to give more influence over your life to others than He is going to give to you. If He is going to stand and judge you by what you do, He is going to give you the authority to make the decision to do it. You cannot use anybody else as an excuse of why you did or did not do what God told you to do. This is why you have to study to show yourself approved. You cannot go to God and start giving excuses. The reason you did not do something cannot be because of so and so, or because of this or that, him or her, or them or it.

Proving the word through another person is not going to be acceptable before God. This is how many former churches operated. Only the preacher had the Bible. Everybody else just listened. Today, you have to study to show yourself approved. I am a pastor and I am not trying to be God for you or anyone. I am trying to lead you to God. I am not trying to tell you what God wants you to do. You have to go find out what He wants you to do, because doing just anything is not going to work.

Galatians 6:3 states, *For if a man think himself to be something, when he is nothing, he deceiveth himself.* We often go to God in faith when God does not need you to go to Him in faith. He needs you to go to Him in truth. You should talk in faith to us and you talk faith to yourself, but you should talk truth to Him. When there is an issue, you need to go to Him in truth. Do not think you are something more than you are when you are not. He already knows what you are. I know you want to give a good perception in your life. You want people to receive you well, but to thine own self be true. You know what you need to work on, so don't say what you do not need to work on. You know what you need to start doing. When you are thinking that you are something that you are not, you are deceiving yourself.

"I don't have a problem with anybody," is what most people say, just as long as nobody is in their face. Avoidance of a problem is not victory. Covering it up is not victory. Denying it when it exists is not victory. The Bible says, *But let every man prove his own work* (Galatians 6:4). Remember, the word *prove* means to verify, test, and establish the truth. *But let every man prove his own work, and then shall he have rejoicing in himself alone, and not in another.*

When I tell you to rejoice with them that rejoice, I want you to rejoice with me, but I want you to have your own works that you can rejoice in yourself too. It is not going to make you any better if I am walking in what I am supposed to walk in, but you are not. It is not going to make you any prosperous if I am doing what I am supposed to be doing and you are not. If you are, then it should be a proven fact. There should be some form of manifestation. There should be some things happening in your life.

1 Thessalonians 5:21 says, *Prove all things; hold fast that which is good.* How do you know if what God is telling you is the truth? How do you know if it is verified? How do you know if it is the genuine thing? How do you know? You have to be willing to prove it and to do it long enough to see the results. If there are no results, then you cannot say this is what God said. If there are no results, then you cannot say this is what God wants me to do. If you are not succeeding in what you say God is telling you to do, then how do you verify and establish the truth that it is what God says? How have you proven Him?

James 1:2-4 says, *My brethren, count it all joy when ye fall into divers temptations; Knowing this, that the trying of your faith worketh patience. But let patience have her perfect work, that ye may be perfect and entire, wanting nothing.* The Amplified Version reads,

> *Consider it wholly joyful, my brethren, whenever you are enveloped in or encounter trials of any sort or fall into various temptations. Be assured and understand that the trial and proving of your faith bring out endurance and steadfastness and patience. But let endurance and steadfastness and patience have full*

> *play and do a thorough work, so that you may be*
> *people perfectly and fully developed with no defects,*
> *lacking in nothing.*

Is not only a good thing to know and do? You have to prove what God is speaking. You have to prove that what God is saying is really what He is saying. Nobody can prove that for you. James 1:12 (Amplified Version) says, *Blessed (happy, spiritually prosperous, favored by God) is the man who is steadfast under trial and perseveres when tempted; for when he has passed the test and been approved, he will receive the [victor's] crown of life which the Lord has promised to those who love Him.* When you stand the test, *then* you are approved. That is why you must study to show yourself that you are equipped, so when the test comes, then you are proved in His word. Just because you study, it does not mean you are approved. Remember, the word is only an assumption until it is proven. It is only proven in the midst of a test. Until you have been tested, then whatever happens is what it is.

First of all, you have to know who you are. This is the issue. We just do not know who we are. Matthew 16:15-16 says, *He saith unto them, But whom say ye that I am? And Simon Peter answered and said, Thou art the Christ, the Son of the living God.* That was the revelation of who He was. If you do not know who He is, how can you become who He is? Christ is not Jesus' last name. Christ is the anointed one and His anointing.

The Anointing on You

If you do not understand the anointing on you, which is what will bring you the victory, you are not going to have any victory. If you do not understand the anointing on you, which is what brings you the power, you are not going to have any power. If you do not understand that the anointing on you is going to give you the right to dominate in this life, then you are not going to dominate. You cannot get the anointing unless you know that you are the son or daughter of God. *For I reckon that the sufferings of this present time are not worthy to be compared with the glory which shall be revealed in us. For the earnest expectation of the creature waiteth for the manifestation of the sons of God* (Romans 8:18-19).

Whatever troubles or tests are coming, they should not be compared to what is going to be revealed in you. God is not talking about the son of Christ. He is talking about us. He is waiting on us to manifest ourselves. All of creation is waiting on us to know who we are. God is never going to put on you an endowment, a power, an ability, or an anointing when you do not know who you are. Matthew 3:13–17 talks about when Jesus was baptized and a voice from heaven said, *"This is my beloved Son, in whom I am well pleased."* Then in Matthew 4, Jesus was led up by the Spirit into the wilderness to be tempted. The Amplified Bible says "tested and tried" by the devil. As soon as heaven declared who He was, the test came to verify who He was. The whole temptation was, "If you are the Son of God, prove it." After the test, you can then say you are who you say you are. Every test is now to see if you are who you say you are.

A test is nothing but pressure to get you to do, or not to do anything other than what God wants. Pressure in any form is to get you to do, or not to do anything other than what God told you to do. God is telling you here comes the test and its purpose is to try to get you to be disobedient to His will. He is telling you not to do something and here comes the test, trying to get you to do it.

Abraham was tested. Genesis 22:1 says, *And it came to pass after these things, that God did tempt Abraham.* In the Amplified Version, it is as follows: *After these events, God tested and proved Abraham.* This is a good thing. It lets me know that Satan does not come before the word, but he comes *for* the word.

There hath no temptation taken you but such as is common to man: but God is faithful, who will not suffer you to be tempted above that ye are able; but will with the temptation also make a way to escape, that ye may be able to bear it (1 Corinthians 10:13). Please believe that you are going to be tested. John 16:33 says, *In the world ye shall have tribulation.* The tribulation is the test.

1 Peter 4:12 says, *Beloved think it not strange concerning fiery trials which is to try you.* How many of you know that the fiery trials are the test? A portion of Matthew 13:21 says, *or when tribulation or persecution ariseth because of the word, by and by he is offended.* How many know that persecution and tribulation are the test, and it arises for the sake of the word? There is a scripture that refers to light and dark occupying the same space (2 Corinthians 6:14). Then why are you so surprised when the devil comes to you when you want to walk in the light? There is a war in which light and dark are at conflict. We are not in the Rodney King environment of, "Why can't we all get along?" It does not work like that. Again, the test is to see if you are really who you say you are. Thou are the son or the daughter of the living God, and I am not talking about what they spoke over Jesus. I am talking about what needs to be spoken over your life. Thou art the Christ the Son, Thou art anointed. How do you know you are anointed? How do you know you are anointed to handle the situation and circumstances that you are facing? You know because He just told you He will not allow you to be tempted or tested above that which you are able to bear. That means that you have the ability to bear this. You have the ability to master this. You have the ability to win this. You are anointed for this. Now you have to believe that you are anointed and you have to believe that you are the son or daughter of God. You must believe that, and the world is waiting for us to manifest ourselves. Read 1 John 5 and you will discover the world will never see Him as He really is until we become who we really are. What made Jesus so awesomely blessed when He walked the earth? The scripture tells us His philosophy, "I do nothing but what the Father tells me to do. I say nothing but what the Father tells me to say. I do not go to any place other than where the Father sends me. When you see me, you see Him. When you know me, you know Him. I did not come to testify of me. I came to testify of Him who sent me." My question is when will the world see Him again? When will people see God, the Father, in you? Until you manifest who He is, the world will never see Him and know Him as He really is.

In verse 4 of 1 John 5, *For whatsoever is born of God overcometh the world: and this is the victory that overcometh the world, even our faith.* Are you born-again? So that means you are born of God, right? So whatsoever is born of God overcomes the world, and this is the victory that overcomes the world, even our faith. Verse 5 states, *Who is he that overcometh the world, but he that believeth that Jesus is the Son of God?* If you do not believe that Jesus is the Son of God, then you will never become the son of God. If you never believe that He walks in what He walked in, then you can never walk in what you need to walk in. If you do not believe that He has the right to dominate on this earth, then you will never believe that you have the right to dominate as a child of God. We say we are children of God, but are we really?

The word *overcome* means to defeat, to conquer, to win, and to master. When you overcome something you have to face it head on. Overcome does not mean to avoid, because avoiding the situation is not victory. Again, avoidance is not victory. You do not have victory when you avoid the conflict. Settle this fact, you are going to have conflict, and you will find yourself having those same conflicts until you decide not to run. You are not overcoming because you are avoiding it. Avoidance is not victory. Victory is to overcome, to defeat, to conquer, to win, and to master. Romans 8:37 says that we are more than conquerors. How can we be more than a conqueror when we have not conquered anything? Is it important that we overcome, or can we keep failing in the same test? Can we be better if we do not overcome? Can we grow if we do not overcome? Can we get to the next level if we do not overcome? If the things that were getting to us before are still getting to us now, can we still get to the next level? If the things that are getting to us now are still getting to us later, can we ever get to a better place? If the things that are getting to us now are still getting to us later, can we ever say that we are growing and maturing? If we are still where we are now and we are going to be the same way later, what is getting better? Can you say I am getting better just because I avoid it? You know I have an issue, so rather than dealing with the issue, I am just going to avoid it. So can I ever get to the next level, can I ever say I am growing in the things of God, if I do not win, defeat, and master that thing? Will the devil always use that against me? The answer is yes. So is it important that we overcome? The answer is still yes!

We are still focused on proving God's word. Revelation 2:7 says, *He that has an ear, let him hear what the Spirit says unto the churches; To him that overcometh to him I give to eat of the tree of life, which is in the midst of the paradise of God.* Do you see this? The tree of life is the reward to those who overcome. So what is it that you have to overcome? Do you have to overcome the test that is in my life? Do you have to overcome the test in somebody else's life? Does that make you an overcomer when you tell me what I need to do and you are not doing what you need to do? What makes you an overcomer? When somebody else's life is made better or when your life is made better? When somebody else does what God says or when you do what God says? When do you become an overcomer? He says to the churches *He that has an ear, let him hear.* We are in that day and time. Verse 11 of Revelation 2 states, *He that hath an ear, let him hear what the Spirit saith unto churches. He that overcometh shall not be hurt over the second death.* Now again, by use of reasoning and understanding, you can make an assumption that if you can overcome, you get the benefits, and you can assume that if you do not overcome, you are not going to get the benefits, because God does not do anything vain, void, and unproductive. Why would He tell you that if you overcome that you are going to get His rewards if you can still get them without overcoming? In verse 17, it says again, *He that hath an ear.* He is putting such an emphasis on us hearing and understanding what needs to happen in these last days. Now again we are talking proving the word and this involves our heart and soul (our chooser and our thinker). You know we are talking about the gates to our hearts (our ears, eyes, and mouth). *He that hath an ear, let him hear what the Spirit saith unto the churches.* He is not talking about a building; He is talking about us. *To him that overcometh will I give to eat of the hidden manna, and will give him a white stone, and in that stone a new name written, which no man knoweth saving he that receiveth it* (Revelation

2:17). Either you are going to receive it or not. Revelation 3:12 reads,

> *Him that overcometh will I make a pillar in the temple of my God, and he shall go no more out: and I will write upon him the name of my God, and the name of the city of my God, which is new Jerusalem, which cometh down out of heaven from my God: and I will write upon him my new name.*

God is continually saying in Revelation that he that has an ear, let him hear what the Spirit says unto the churches. So is it necessary to overcome, and again what are we talking about when we say overcome? I am talking about the test that you are facing. I am talking about the situation that you are in the midst of. I am talking about those issues that you still deal with, because you cannot go any farther unless you overcome them. You cannot get to another level without overcoming the issue. We cannot do any more and you have not proven the word. Why not? It has not been proven because if you are who you say you are, there would not be an issue. If you do what He tells you, according to Revelation 3:21, this will be the result: *To him that overcometh will I grant to sit with me in my throne, even as I also overcame.* You cannot be like Jesus if you do not overcome, because as He overcame, you need to overcome. I am not talking about the same situations. Whatever He faced He overcame. We all have different walks. We have different functions. We have different callings, different destinies, but we all are still required to overcome in order to get His rewards. You can never get to the place that God wants you to get to. If He says you have to press toward the mark, *pressing* means that there is something that is going to try to prevent you. If you say that this present suffering could not be compared to the glory that shall be revealed, then it means that the present situation is not the end and that the glory that you are expecting should be the end. However, the glory expected will not be manifested if you do not go through it.

Let us study the last point in Revelation 3:21 which puts an emphasis on the necessity to overcome. If you look in the Bible, all of the other scriptures I cited were in the red and that means Jesus was the one who was talking. However Revelation 21:7 is not in the red, so Jesus is not talking here. Then who is talking? *He that overcometh shall inherit all things: and I will be his God, and he shall my son* (Revelation 21:7). It is our Father, God who gives the last word about the importance of being an overcomer.

Jesus asked His disciples whom did they think He was. Peter answered the He was the Christ, the Son of the living God. So who do people think you are? If you are a son or daughter of the living God then prove it. You know in Genesis, the Bible says every kind reproduces after his own kind. God said, "I overcame." Jesus said, "I am a chip off the old block and I overcame." Then God said, "I want you to be my sons and daughters. I want you to inherit my kingdom. I want you to rule and reign." That means you have to overcome as well. In Luke 6:47 Jesus said, *Whosoever cometh to me, and heareth my sayings, and doeth them, and I will shew you to whom he is like.* Is He speaking as the Son or is He giving us the Father's words? Think about it. Remember the statement Jesus said and that I keep telling you? *I say nothing other than what the Father tells me to say. I do nothing other than what the Father tells me to do. I go no place other than what the Father tells me to go. When you see Me, you see Him. When you know Me, you know Him. When you hear me, you hear Him.* So is He giving you what the Son says, or is He telling you what the Father's words say? When we tell others what God wants them to know, are we speaking as sons and daughters or are we giving them the Father's words? See it does not matter, in my opinion, if I am a son or daughter, but it matters what God wants them to know. Okay, so He is saying, *Whosoever come to me and heareth the Father's saying and doeth them, I will show him to whom he is like: He is like a man which built an house and digged deep, and laid the foundation on a rock: and when the flood arose* (the struggles, the tests), *the stream beat vehemently upon the house, and could not shake it: for it was founded upon a rock* (Luke 6:47–48). *And upon this rock, I will build my church* (Matthew 16:18).

So my question to you again is, are you the son or daughter of the living God? Are you really who you say you are, and if you are, then prove it. How do you prove it? You have to pass the test. You cannot say, "I am who I am," and then every test that comes, you are still subject to it.

Here is an exercise for you to do. I want you to find the word you say you are doing to see if it is capable of being done. You see, most of the words that are in the Bible are not for you to do; but they are for you to understand the mind-set you need to possess. Remember, most of the words that are in the Bible for you to do are general; you still have to go to God to get to the specifics. We learned about this. I am going to give you a scripture. In fact, I am going to give you several scriptures right now. My favorite scripture, Philippians 4:13, which is the one my ministry is based on, is *I can do all things through Christ which strengthens me.* How do you do that, or is that the mind-set you have when He tells you what to do? *No weapon formed against me shall prosper. And every tongue that rises up shall be condemned.* How do you do that, or is that the mind-set you have when somebody speaks against you? What you do is what He tells you specifically from the Father. Otherwise, the scriptures are to show you the attitude and mind-set to have when He tells you specifics.

How do you do this? How do you do, *thou shall love thy neighbor as thyself?* Now you can do that one, but understand that this is a general statement. Yet does it tell you which neighbor to love and how to love them? You have to get the "how-to" and the "who-to" instructions specifically from the Father. You cannot just love them, because again, if it is just *love thy neighbor as thyself,* He also said for you to *love your enemies, too.* You should love everybody. We can generalize it and love everybody who includes our neighbor, but when He says *love thy neighbor as you love thyself,* He is really saying that there are some specific things He wants you to do. You are going to be told by Him that *you are going to make a difference in them,* but you are not going to read this statement specifically in the word. You are going to hear *that one* in a relationship. You see, the written word is going to get you to Him and He is going to tell you how to live.

This is what I want you to do, take all the word that you have been standing on, everything you say you have been doing, and write them down. Then write down how you have been doing them. See if these words are something you can do or something that you should be thinking, and the mind-set you should have before He tells you what to do.

It must be what He tells you to do that is going to cause manifestation. It is time to get the result, and to overcome. It is time to start manifesting who you are by saying, "Father, tell me specifically what to do, and I will do it." *That* is the glory, hope, and expectation that we have which assures us that we are going to get beyond where we are. Who do men say that you are? Pass the test. Establish the truth. Verify his words that He is speaking. Be willing to prove it by doing it. Are you ready?

CHAPTER 5

The Holy Spirit—Developing the Body

Who You Yield Your Member To

We have come to the third aspect in *Developing the Complete You*. Recall how it has been established from when God said, *Let us make man in our image and in our own likeness*. God is a spirit, and He possesses God the Father, God the Son, and God the Holy Spirit. This is the fullness of God made up of the triune parts of God. Man is a spirit; he possesses a soul, and lives in a body. Remember that each part of God develops a different part of man, and it has to be done in the right order to maximize God's ability. The word *maximize* is essential because you cannot achieve the maximum potential for the God in you until you become more specific about God in you.

I am ready to see the fullness of God's manifestation in this lifetime. I am ready for the world to see Him as He really is. Yet this is not going to happen if we are still general in our thinking, if we are still vague in our approach toward life, and if we allow just anything to be good enough versus allowing the best to be the best. So we have to make sure that our whole intention is the relationship with the Father because that relationship is everything. Relationship is why man was created initially in Genesis. The thing that was interrupted by sin when Adam disobeyed is the relationship with the Father. The thing that Jesus came to redeem back for man was the relationship and the access to the Father. The benefit of Jesus is the access He provides to the Father. He is here to make us think more in line with the Father's will for our life. We have got to know that, believe that, and take advantage of that benefit. The words in the Bible were written so that you can use them to stabilize your way of thinking. After we know how to think, then we can obey the specifics of what the Father is telling us. Then the manifestations will prove to all who see that we are who we say we are.

Now we are going to get to the third and last portion: how the Holy Spirit develops the body. This is the easiest part once the spirit and the mind are functioning in the proper order. When we talk about the Spirit of God on our flesh, we must realize that the Spirit of God on the flesh is the anointing on our lives. The Holy Spirit on our flesh is the supernatural ability to do what we could not do before He came. It is essential to believe and renew your mind so you can experience this supernatural ability in your life.

Renewing the mind leads you to the Father, yet most believers still go through life with an unrenewed mind, and the majority of the time, that unrenewed mind caters to the flesh instead of allowing the Spirit of God to govern its actions. Did you realize that the body does not do anything on its own? Please know that anything that you are doing, you did not do it accidentally. You had a thought first and you planned it. It may have been a quick thought, but it was still a thought. Your body does not operate independently of itself. If that were the case, then why is a person who is brain dead not able to do anything? A brain-dead person will just lie there even though he is still kept alive on life support. Since there is no brain activity, the body will not respond. Again, your body does not do anything independently of itself. So that means something has to be governing it. With that thought, we are going to study and discover who you are yielding your members to, because it is all about you yielding your body to obedience.

Romans 6:1-2 says, *What shall we say then? Shall we continue in sin, that grace may abound? God forbid. How shall we, that are dead to sin, live any longer therein?* If we are dead to sin, why should we desire to live in sin? Christians need to get to the point where they understand that choosing to live in the sin life is not the best life. How many of you believe that after Adam sinned he realized that he made a mistake? We can all relate to the feeling of doing something wrong and then saying, "I shouldn't have done that." You cannot (or should not) make a mistake and think the mistake is the best thing that you should have done, then say, "If I had the choice again, I will make the same decision." That is crazy!

I am trying to get you to understand that when you know something is a sin, you cannot believe that the sin is the right way and the right path to take. If that is so, then you *want* to live in the sin. Those who believe that they have been bought out of and delivered from sin should not desire to go back to it. Even if you find yourself falling into it, there should not be a desire to continue in that sin. Just because we are under grace and our sin is covered, we should not say, "Let me go ahead and do it anyway." Our sin is covered, but we still should not desire to commit sin. This is why renewing the mind is so important, because you are never going to change your action until you change your mind. You are never going to change your action until you change how you think about the action. *Know ye not, that so many of us as were baptized into Jesus Christ were baptized into his death? Therefore we are buried with him by baptism unto death: that like as Christ was raised up from the dead by the glory of the Father, even so we also should walk in newness of life* (Romans 6:3-4).

Let me say again that a renewed mind leads you to the Father, but an unrenewed mind, most of the time, caters to the flesh. When you do not embrace the newness of life, you are going to embrace your old way of doing and your old way of thinking. This you should not do. You are not just performing an act because you are just doing it; you are performing an act because you are thinking it. The act is what you want to do.

For if we have been planted together in the likeness of his death, we shall also be in the likeness of his resurrection: knowing this, that our old man is crucified with him, that the body of sin might be destroyed, that henceforth we should not serve sin. For he that is dead is freed from sin (Romans 6:5–7). His death represented the old way of living in sin, being put under subjection. If we embrace His resurrection, we can also embrace His death. You cannot embrace His resurrection unless you embrace His death. You cannot embrace the deliverance to the new life you ought to live if you have not embraced the death of the old life you used to live. You are still trying to live the dead life in your born-again state, which is your new life. In other words, you are trying to live the past and the present, the old and the new, and you cannot do that. One of them has to die, because one will negatively affect each other.

Romans 6:8–10 states, *Now if we be dead with Christ, we believe that we shall also live with him: Knowing that Christ being raised from the dead dieth no more; death hath no more dominion over him. For in that he died, he died unto sin once: but in that he liveth, he liveth unto God.* I am trying to get you to understand that the act is secondary to your mind-set. If your mind is being renewed, it is going to lead to the Father, and the Father is going to lead you back to doing the things you need to do right in your body. However, if your mind is not renewed, then you are going to continue to struggle, going around those same mountains, dealing with those same issues, and still having those same consequences in life that you always had because you did not change the way you have been thinking.

Now this part may be a little uncomfortable to admit. Romans 6:11–13 says, *Likewise reckon ye also yourselves to be dead indeed unto sin, but alive unto God through Jesus Christ our Lord. Let not sin therefore reign in your mortal body, that ye should obey it in the lusts thereof. Neither yield ye your members as instruments of unrighteousness unto sin.* I realize that it is about the act, and the work is from yielding. Who are you yielding to? What are you yielding to? I think there is a song, "Yield Not unto Temptation for It Is Sin." The acid test of who you are yielding to is revealed by your actions. I can tell where you are in your walk with God based on your actions. Oh, you can say all you want to say. You can even believe all you want to believe, but when you are squeezed what you do is the reality of who you are.

Romans 6:13–16 states, *Neither yield ye your members as instruments of unrighteousness unto sin: but yield yourselves unto God, as those that are alive from the dead, and your members as instruments of righteousness unto God. For sin shall not have dominion over you: for ye are not under the law, but under grace. What then? shall we sin, because we are not under the law, but under grace? God forbid. Know ye not, that to whom ye yield yourselves servants to obey, his servants ye are to whom ye obey; whether of sin unto death, or of obedience unto righteousness?*

This is how I can tell where you are. Who are you obeying? I am not talking about what you are saying; I am not talking about what you are thinking. I am not talking about what you believe in; I am talking about what you are *doing*, because who you are obeying is who you are serving.

Here is where it gets better in Romans 6:17–19.

> *But God be thanked, that ye were the servants of sin, but ye have obeyed from the heart that form of doctrine which was delivered you. Being then made free from sin, ye became the servants of righteousness. I speak after the manner of men because of the infirmity of your flesh, for as ye have yielded your members servants to uncleanness and to iniquity unto iniquity; even so now yield your members servants to righteousness unto holiness.*

You *can* do what God wants. If you could not do what was written, then He would not have told you to do so. You can obey God because you can make a choice; you just have to choose. Choose what? Choose the way, think the truth, and experience the life. That is why in Proverbs 3:5–6 it says to *Trust in the Lord with all thine heart; and lean not unto thine own understanding. In all thy ways acknowledge him, and he shall direct thy paths.* He cannot direct you on a path that you do not want to go. He cannot direct you on a path that you have not chosen. If you do not choose His way, then Him directing you will not work.

Verses 20–21 of Romans 6 says, *For when ye were the servants of sin, ye were free from righteousness. What fruit had ye then in those things whereof ye are now ashamed? for the end of those things is death.* Or, perhaps, you are not ashamed. If you were ashamed, then you would not keep doing the old ways. You have to believe if you do the old ways consistently, then it is going to produce the same rotten fruit. Verse 22–23 ends the chapter with this thought: *But now being made free from sin, and become servants to God, ye have your fruit unto holiness, and the end everlasting life. For the wages of sin is death; but the gift of God is eternal life through Jesus Christ our Lord.* Realize that it is all about being yielded. How much can you yield?

The Greatest Evidence

Since we are discussing being yielded, let us examine the baptism of the Holy Spirit and how it pertains to yielding. I am like the apostle Paul who said, "I thank God that I pray in tongues more than you all." However, it is not just primarily about the act of praying in tongues. Speaking in tongues is the evidence of your baptism in the Holy Spirit; unfortunately, the gift of speaking in tongues seems to have reduced the Spirit of God just to this form of evidence. Some may believe that if a believer does not speak in tongues, then that person does not have the baptism of the Holy Spirit. In reality, the baptism of the Holy Spirit is one out of many ways a person can yield to the Spirit of God to do something one could not do before, such as speaking in another unfamiliar language.

The reason He wants believers to pray in tongues is because when we pray, what we say is important. Yet let me tell you something, for the most part what you say does not do anything except be a tool to convince yourself and others. If I say something long enough, I believe it, and if others hear it long enough, they may believe it. The ultimate tool to convince others to believe is if we *do* what we say, because the greatest evidence of the Spirit of God on your flesh is not what you speak; it is what you do. So here is the question, if I do not speak a word in tongues, but I do what the Spirit asks me to do, then am I still baptized? So how much can you yield to?

Speaking is secondary to doing, and speaking is not the substitute for doing. Love, belief, faith, trust, and obedience, are all judged by your actions, not by your words. God so loved the world that He gave, so the love that you have is based on what He did and not just on what He said. Your belief is not based primarily on what you think or on what you say you believe. Your belief is verified in your actions. Your faith without works is dead. Your faith is verified in your actions. Trusting in the Lord with all your heart and leaning not to your own understanding is proven in your actions. Your obedience is solidified by your actions, not by merely acknowledging what you heard. You cannot say you are obeying God, and your actions show that you are not obeying Him. In other words, what you are doing is sin if you are doing the opposite of this certain action that He wants.

Let me bring you back to this point; in order to have the Spirit of God, or the anointing on your life, your mind needs to be renewed; and renewing your mind will always lead you back to the Father. Do you remember the WWJD fashion trend where people wore a bracelet with that acronym, which means What Would Jesus Do? I believe a more accurate and helpful thing to get God's results across would have been HWJT, How Would Jesus Think? Think about that; how *would* Jesus *think*? What would Jesus do is not how Jesus operated because whatever Jesus did was what the Father told Him to. However, if you have this mind in you that is also in Christ Jesus, then the question would be, "What would Jesus think about this?" Then our response would be the same as Jesus' and we would allow the Father to tell us what to do.

Some people believe we cannot live as Jesus did because, after all, Jesus is God. Yet I want you to ponder this for a moment; have you ever noticed that you can do *whatever* you really want to do? Proverbs 23:7 states, *As a man thinketh in his heart, so is he.* If you want to do something bad enough, you will find a way. Do not tell me what you cannot do; just tell me what you do not want to do, because when you want to do something bad enough, you will find a way. You can get any house, any car, or anything else you want if you want it bad enough. This is because you will be willing to do whatever it takes to get it. It may not be the will of God, but you will still do it.

Please do not misunderstand me. Having what you want or doing what you want is not all bad, but it is when we do not allow these desires to be used for the good all the time. In other words, I can do anything I really want to do, but I just need to change what I want to do. I need to change it to line up with what God wants, and change starts with the three *d's*: decision, discipline, and delight. The three *d's* are to make a quality decision, discipline yourself to do it, and then be delighted in doing it. The Bible states that we should ultimately get to that place of delight. Psalms 37:4 says, *Delight thyself also in the Lord: and he shall give thee the desires of thine heart.* We want to get to that place of delight, because we want to see the manifestation and the fullness of God. We want to see results. Now, I am not going to split hairs on whose desires, because when you get to the place of delight, you are already going to know that it is God's desires in you that you desire. So you can debate my desire or God's desire; but to be quite honest with you, you are never going to get to the place of delight until it is already figured out. Once you are in delight, whose desire it is will not be an issue, because you will know it is God's desire.

We are still talking about God's Spirit developing your spirit, and this is the thing you have to understand; if you are trying to get to the area of delight, you can only come to it through the way of discipline. If you are trying to get to discipline, you can only come to it by the way of you making a decision. Decision empowers you to achieve discipline; discipline empowers you to reach delight, and your delight empowers you to obtain increases or results (God's Spirit on you). Please settle that if you are *not* seeing God's results, then it is because you are choosing things that God is not enforcing because these are not God's desires for you. You want these things, and based on what your thinking is, the Holy Spirit will never override your decisions.

I am trying to convince you to change from *your* thinking; and you know I am linking your thinking to your actions so that when we start talking about your actions, you do not forsake how you think.

The Purpose of the Spirit

We have been so slothful when it comes to the Spirit of God. We make the decision to do what we want and presume he is going to back up our decision. Thus, we use Him as an errand boy. We use Him as a step and fetch it. We use Him as a crutch. We try to use Him as a substitute for what we can do. He is never going to do exactly what you can do. He will do more than what you can do when you finish *all* that you can do. The Holy Spirit is there to empower the action of how you think and what you think when it lines up with the will of God. The Holy Spirit is there to empower how you feel when it lines up with the will of God. In other words, if you are thinking something that does not line up with the will of God, the Holy Spirit is not going to empower you to do *that*. Now you can accomplish most of what you want without the assistance of the Holy Spirit, because you have done it before. Again, you cannot tell me that you cannot do or achieve certain things. You can do certain things like staying up late or getting up early when you really want to, but the spirit of God is not going to empower you to do something when it is not God's will. He is not going to put an endowment on you when it is not going to make you better and especially when it is not God's will.

You have done a lot of things on your own without the endorsement of the Holy Spirit, but then when it comes to the Holy Spirit and what He wants, you are limited. How can that be? It is because you are not in agreement with what God wants; you just want it to happen without any participation on your part. Just think about all the things you have gotten yourself into and how those experiences took a lot of effort and materials for you to get there. Some of you have purchased big houses and big cars on your own. You have acquired a lot of stuff on your own. How much have you and the Holy Spirit achieved? He is supposed to empower you to do better than what you can do on your own, but He is not going to empower you to do something outside of God's will. He is never going to start something in you until you get to your end.

So, we are going to continue to talk about this in chapter 6. However, I want to end chapter 5 with this prevailing thought. There is one particular word in this next verse that I want to emphasize, and that word is *helpeth.* According to Romans 8:26, *Likewise the Spirit also helpeth our infirmities: for we know not what we should pray for as we ought: but the Spirit itself maketh intercession for us with groanings which cannot be uttered.* This is what God showed me. You want the anointing and the Spirit of God to empower you to do something, but the Spirit of God is saying, "What you want to do is not God's will. Let me help you find out God's will because I am not going to empower you to do anything other than that."

CHAPTER 6

The Holy Spirit Developing the Body

Endowed with Power

In chapter 5, we discussed the importance of renewing the mind to think as Jesus would and allow God to give us direction and for us to obey that direction. Only when we have made the decision to be disciplined and delight in God's way will the Holy Spirit provide His assistance to help us accomplish God's desires or, in other words, His will. God's manifestation can often be referred to as *glory*. Isaiah 60:1 says, *Arise, shine; for thy light is come, and the glory of the Lord is risen upon thee.* Let the glory of God rise upon us! That is what we want and what has to happen.

Unfortunately, some believers think that glory upon them does not matter. Some think that what we do can just be "whatever," but know that *glory* has to be the fullness of God's word being seen and evident in our lives. This is the verification of God being real in our lives. We can say it, we can believe it, we can share it, but until we show it, then it has not been proven. I believe what people hear, they understand, but what they see, they believe. We are not trying to get people to just understand. We are trying to get them to believe. When it is all said and done, the only real thing that is going to last and the only true thing that is going to exist is God's word. Our lives should be a testimony that there is no other way but God's way. His way will be the best way. Amen.

Developing the Complete You is very important because I really believe that God is building and doing something great and mighty through us and for us. He is preparing a better and more awesome foundation because of what He wants to do, and what He always intended to do is not just in our lives only. Let me share something with you; you are not the first person that has received the call of God on your life. If you are not going to do it because you are not willing to do it, you can believe that you will not be the last person He tells to do it. The things that He wants to do through you He has wanted to do through others as well. I believe God has found a group of people that will allow it to happen, and that is the answer. Has God expressed His desire enough to you that you are convinced and will yield to allow it to be done? The only thing that is holding the return of Jesus back is that everything that He wants to be done has not been done, and unless we do it, He is not going to come because it has to be done.

Since He said, *So shall my word be that goeth forth out of my mouth: it shall not return unto me void, but it shall accomplish that which I please, and it shall prosper in the thing whereto I sent it* (Isaiah 55:11), He means that not one word of His will return unto Him vain, void, or unproductive, but it will accomplish what He sent it to accomplish. That means if He tells you that word and you do not do it, then He is going to tell that word to somebody else so that it can be done. You have work to do, and it has to happen. So this is why we are going to develop the complete you! For too long we have been eating the crumbs under the table and not sitting at the table and eating the full meal. We are seeing only a portion of what God can do because we have not truly allowed God to do all that He wants to do.

It is time for us to stop being so general in the things of God and be very specific in order to maximize the full potential of God. Hopefully after reading this book, you will no longer put God in this generic box, but recognize Him as a unique and distinct triune being: God the Father, God the Son, and God the Holy Spirit. After this study, you will want to maximize the fullness of God, and you will be more specific about who or which part of God you are dealing with. You will know who you are talking to or seeking or yielding to in order for the fullness to manifest.

God is ready to release the fullness of what He has for us, as we continue to develop our spirit man by maintaining a personal relationship with the father. We learned that through Jesus, we have regained total access back to our heavenly Father. We realize that our minds are renewed and developed by the intimate relationship and through our study of Jesus the word. That is how we change our thinking, because Jesus is only a bridge, a door, and a pathway to the Father. You will never maximize Jesus' full potential if you do not take advantage of the relationship with the Father.

Now we are at the last part, which is developing our physical man by the Spirit of God, which is the Spirit of God on the flesh. That is the easiest part of development, and most of the time, that is the part we want to focus on. The anointing of God will come upon us when we are seeking the first two stages of development. When you are seeking the relationship with the Father and renewing our mind with the Son, then the Spirit of God will come on the flesh to give you the ability that you did not have before. So when talking about developing the physical part of man we have to address being *endowed* with power, because that is what the Spirit wants to do. To *endow* means to equip with a quality or talent. He wants to equip you with power. He wants to place ability on you that you did not have before He came in you and upon you.

We are going to study being endowed by reading in the book of Joel. I want to start from the Old Testament because it is a foretelling of the prophecy of what is going to happen in the New

Testament. It foretold about the birth of Jesus and all that is related to Jesus. So you have to realize that what He is telling you in Joel is what is going to happen in the New Testament.

Joel 2:28–29 says, *It is shall come pass afterward.* How many of you know that afterward has come to pass? Or it should have. That means we should be in the afterward, and we should not be waiting on this. *It should come to pass afterward that I will pour out my Spirit upon all flesh; and your sons and your daughters shall prophesy, your old men shall dream dreams, your young men shall see visions. And also upon the servants and the handmaidens in those days will I pour out my spirit.*

So we understand that He is saying in the Old Testament that He wants to pour out His Spirit upon all flesh. When we understand what is going to happen and when that takes place, we should know what to expect and what to be walking in. Let us look at Acts 1:6–8, and see when it happens.

> *When they therefore were come together, they asked of him, saying, Lord, wilt thou at this time restore again the kingdom of Israel? And he said unto them, It is not for you to know the times or the seasons, which the Father hath put in his own power. But ye shall receive power, after that the Holy Ghost is come upon you: and ye shall be witnesses unto me both in Jerusalem, and in all Judaea, and in Samaria, and unto the uttermost part of the earth.*

It is written, *But ye shall receive power after that.* When shall you receive power? *After that* is when the Holy Ghost is come *upon* you. He did not say after the Holy Ghost has come *in you*, you got it? You were not endowed with power when you got saved. Also, speaking in tongues is not the fullness of the power. It says *with the evidence of speaking in tongues* which means that you have yielded to the power in some form or fashion. As I stated previously in chapter 5, most Christians limit the yielding to the power to just the speaking in tongues. Rather, speaking in tongues should only be your sign and a sign to others that you have yielded yourself to the Spirit of God in what you do. If you just limit what He can do through you to just speaking in tongues, then you have limited Him and He has not come on you.

Think of being baptized in the Spirit of God as being totally submerged. It means when you speak in tongues, you are totally submerged; and when you quit speaking in tongues, He still wants you totally submerged. This means when you are talking to folks, you are totally submerged because the power of God is on you when you speak. When you are dealing with people, you are totally submerged because when you act in what you are doing, you are equipped and empowered by Him. This is what it means when you are baptized, not just when you are speaking in tongues. You do not have to speak in tongues to be baptized in the Spirit. *Baptized* means I am yielding and the endowment of power has come upon me. That means I am doing what the Spirit empowered me to do, so I am baptized. Please do not have this misunderstanding. Do not make a religion out of it. Some people are criticizing and condemning folks who do not speak in tongues, and they who are being put down have more power on their lives than those who speak in tongues. Again, speaking in tongues is only one aspect of His power.

Anyway, *you are going to receive power when the spirit of God comes upon you.* You are not going to receive power when you speak in tongues. *And shall be witnesses to me both in Jerusalem and all Judea, Samaria, and unto the uttermost part of the earth.* Please realize that you cannot be a witness unless the power is there on your life. Again, speaking in tongues is one form of evidence; doing something you cannot do is also evidence. Saying something that you did not understand or something that went past your brain is also evidence. Acting in a way that is not natural in you but is the way of the Spirit of God upon you is the evidence. Not living a life above your means, but living a life in His means is also evidence of the power coming upon you. How much evidence do you have? Let me *see* how much of the Holy Ghost is upon you. If there is no evidence, then He is not upon you.

The Anointing

Acts 10:38 reads, *How God anointed Jesus of Nazareth with the Holy Ghost and with power: who went about doing good, and healing all that were oppressed of the devil; for God was with him.* I want to introduce that word *anointed*, which means *up on*, right? We call it the anointing; that burden removing, yoke destroying power, and that supernatural ability upon the flesh. *I shall pour out my spirit upon the flesh. How God anointed Jesus of Nazareth with the Holy Ghost, the Spirit of God.* Do you see who anoints the individual? It was God which in turn is the Holy Ghost aspect of Him. God *anointed Jesus of Nazareth with the Holy Ghost and power who went about doing good and healing all that was oppressed of the devil for God was with Him.* Again, which part of God did the work? It was the Holy Ghost that came with the power, or the ability to get results.

According to 1 John 2:20, you have the unction from the Holy One and you know all things. What is the unction from the Holy Ghost? That is the anointing and the empowerment. What *all things* do you know? Where to go, what to say, and what to do. Again, He is never going to anoint you until you know what to say, you know where to go, and you know what to do. The unction is an empowerment for what He is wanting. When the Father tells you to do something and then you think about it; then you will receive the empowerment to do it. You cannot get an anointing to do what you do not know. Think of it in these terms, if you do not have an anointing for something, then it means you do not have a word for that "something." If you do have a word for "something," then you have the anointing for it. So do not look for the anointing, look for the word. Look for what He tells you to do, and with the word comes the anointing and the ability to do it.

I want you to yield yourself to the Spirit of God upon the flesh. If God tells you to do something and your mind is thinking in line with what Jesus' mind-set was, that means you are totally submitted to do what the Father tells you to do. You should have the mind-set of "I say what the Father tells me to say. I go where the

Father tells me to go. All I need to know is what to say, what to do, and where to go, and then the empowerment will come upon me for that." Remember the endowment comes for you to accomplish God's will for what to say, what to do, and where to go.

In times past, we have been trying to get the ability before we get the word, but with the word comes the ability. He is never going to anoint you to do what He has not told you to do. That is the thing that I try to get people to understand. You never get Him to follow you. You will have to follow Him. You know you can go and pray for whatever you want, but He is not going to move. He is not going to release, and He is not going to provide what is not His will for your life. Neither will He provide that which is not going to be beneficial for your life. He knows your timing. He knows your readiness, and He knows His purpose for your life. Until all that lines up, He is not going to release the power to do it.

Verse 27 of the same chapter states, *But the anointing which ye have received of him abideth in you, and ye need not that any man teach you: but as the same anointing teacheth you of all things, and is truth, and is no lie, and even as it hath taught you, ye shall abide in him.*

According to this, the anointing abides or lives in you. Therefore, you do not have to look for the power and the ability outside of you. If you are being defeated by outside forces, then I will tell you what I tell the congregation that I pastor. *If people, situations, and circumstances have that much influence over you, it is because God does not have enough influence over you.* When the Holy Spirit, who is in you, has more influence in you than the things around you, then you are going to affect the things around you. Yet when you are more influenced by the things around you than by the Holy Spirit that is in you, then you are going to be subject to the people, the situations, or the circumstances.

When you realize that the Spirit of God that abides in you is the anointing, power, and ability to get results, then you are not going to look for the answer, you are going to let the answer *be* you. *But the anointing you have received from Him abides in you and you do not need any man to teach you.* What does this statement mean?

Is it that you do not need to be taught *anything* or you do not need to be taught what to do? Some may think, "I do not need any man to teach me." What this means is that you do not need any man to teach you what God told you to do. That is the only thing He is talking about.

According to scripture, the anointing is put in you to do. You just need to yield to that. However, does the same anointing teach you *all things*? What *all things* does He teach you? He does not teach you literally *everything*. Most of us who believe have some degree of anointing operating in our lives, but does that particular anointing give us the ability to know *everything*? The answer to that is no; the anointing that we have on our lives gives us the ability to know the purpose we are anointed for.

I am trying to get you to not get so super deep, so spiritually deep that you are no earthly good. You cannot be so "out there" that you are not thinking soberly and in line with what God has called you to do. You see, I cannot do what God did not call me or anoint me to do. I am not trying to do that, and neither can you. It does not matter if there is a legitimate need in the life of someone; if you are not the person, the instrument, or the vessel that God wants to use, then you are not getting the anointing to be anything for that person. What I am saying is that you cannot do anything and everything because it is not at "all cost." God is not so desperate that He wants things to happen that He will use anything and anyone at all cost. No, He is going to anoint who He wants for what He wants to happen.

God is purposeful and there is a reason for everything He does. When the anointing is on your life, it is for a twofold purpose: it is to get a result and to develop you. He is never going to develop you for something that He has not called you to do. Again, He is all about purpose, so that means whatever He has done in your past, it is a foundation for what He is doing now, which will be a foundation for what He is going to do later. He is building precept upon precept. He has never done anything or put anything in you that was not useful and will not benefit you right now. He does not take away and replace it with something else. He adds upon what

He has already established. You must believe this. So if He did not call you to do a certain thing, then He is not going to anoint you to do it, because to anoint you to do it would be developing you for a purpose that He has not predestined you to walk in.

Some of you may be questioning in your minds, "Well, what about grace?" Okay, what about grace? What do we know about grace? Does grace come just because we want something to happen, or does grace come because of what we think God wants to happen even when it is wrong? The answer to this question comes down to what we believe God wants for our lives. Grace and mercy does not cover us when we know doing a certain thing is wrong. When we know that it is not the will of God for our lives, grace and mercy does not cover us. Consequences will happen. Mercy and grace cover us when we believe and think with all our hearts that this is what God wants, even though in reality it is not. God's grace and mercy covering us when we are trying to do what He wants is God's way of saying that it is all right and that He is looking at your heart.

Anointed for a Purpose

It is essential that we find out the will of God or the purpose of God for our lives? Or the things that God is preparing us to do? Should we just live a life of "Que sera, sera, whatever will be, will be? The future's not ours to see, que sera, sera?" Is that all right? Is that enough? Can we do that? Can we just encounter anything and accept anything? Is it not God's will for us to know before time what He is preparing us for? God does want us to know and not be caught off guard by situations and circumstances. Being prepared is a part of growing up and maturing; as you grow and mature, you gain more insight. When you are immature, God is not going to show you a whole lot because you cannot handle a whole lot; but as you develop and mature, He is going to show you your destiny, and He is going to show you how each step has been prepared for you to reach your destiny.

God does not want you to be caught up in the letter of the law, but to be led by His Spirit. God may show you the end from the beginning, but He still wants and needs to lead you in each step. For example, someone once asked me a question about a business he had and he was uncertain about God's direction. He asked, "When am I going to know if it's God or not?" I told him that God may have told him to start but not to finish it, but he saw what God told him to start and he assumed that God wanted him to finish. Now he is determined not to stop until he finishes it when God is trying to stop him along the way. That is what happens to many Christians. God showed you four steps, but He wants to guide you in each step, so you need to stop. You have taken two steps and the Spirit is trying to get you to pause, but you are still stuck on taking four steps because that is what you saw. God wants you to stop now, so stop! Okay, now that you have followed instructions, you can take the other two as the Spirit leads. That is the type of obedience He wants; not having presumption on our part. Again, many of us do not understand that we cannot be stuck on one set of instructions because we will miss out on something else God wants us to develop in and accomplish. You cannot have the attitude of, "God showed me the whole thing, and I am set on that."

A perfect example provided in the Bible that illustrates this concept is when Jesus was going to the house of Jairus to heal his daughter. In the midst of going, He was interrupted by the woman with the issue of blood. He could have said no because He already had an assignment from God; we know that because of what He said, *I do not do anything but what the Father told me to do.* So we can conclude the Father must have told Him to go to Jairus's house. Yet in the midst of this, He was still able to hear and obey God to stop and do something different when He helped the woman with the issue of blood. Some of you hear the first word God told you, but you do not hear anything after that. To be endowed with power, we should always have an ear to hear what the Spirit of God is directing us to do.

John 5:21 states, *For as the father raiseth up the dead, and quickeneth them; even so the Son quickeneth whom he will.* The

Amplified Version reads *Just as the Father raises the dead and gives them life [and allows them to live on], even so the Son also gives life to whom He wishes.* To *quicken* means to make alive; the anointing is to quicken you. It is to make alive that which is dead or that which is lying dormant. Another scripture that verifies this is Romans 8:11 which reads, *But if the spirit of him that raised up Jesus from the dead dwell in you, he that raised up Christ from the dead shall also quicken your mortal bodies by his Spirit that dwelleth in you.* I wanted you to read that one so that you can see the definition. To quicken something is to bring life to it. This is the point I want you to grasp; you are never going to see the life God has for you if you are not being quickened or if you are not anointed with God's Spirit. The Holy Spirit shall make alive, should endue you with power and shall bring the ability and anointing to get results.

It does not matter how you were before you got saved or before you got the Spirit of God upon you. Now that the Spirit of God is upon you, you are different. I do not understand how we as Christian people, children of the most of High God, still live our lives subject to situations, events, and people. He has quickened our mortal bodies, so we are not the same. What we were subject to before we received the new birth, we are not subject to now. Why? The answer is because we have a greater ability upon us that we did not have before He came in us. If you are still the same way and subject to the same things as you were before He came, what was the benefit of Him coming? What is the ability in you if He cannot get on you?

The Inner Man

Let us look at Ephesians 3, because some of you have heard what God wants you to do. You just have not yielded to the Spirit of God in you so that He can come upon you in order for you to have the ability to get the job done. Ephesians 3:16 says, *That he would grant you, according to the riches of his glory, to be strengthened with might by his Spirit in the inner man.* Do you see this? That He will grant you according to riches of *whose* glory? We have come back full circle to the beginning of this chapter where I made this statement, "Let the glory of the Lord rise upon us." We can make that happen; but how is it going to happen? *That He will grant you according to the riches of His glory to be strengthened with might by His spirit in the inner man.* It is all there in your inner man. You have the ability to manifest God's glory, to do God's will, and to perform God's word for your life. At times when God speaks to me in my inner man I do not fully understand the revelation. Many times you may not understand all of what God is speaking to you. You may only have a portion of the understanding, but with development and maturity in what you need to understand with more revelation it should come to you.

I never fully understood the fullness of the revelation that God gave me when I was serving my pastor, Dr. Creflo Dollar of World Changers Church International. Yet the understanding of the revelation I had empowered me. The revelation was that my anointing came from his command. I understood that if I could not do something before Dr. Dollar asked, I could do it because he asked. I receive my pastor's command as a word from God, and God would not ask me to do something that He would not empower me to do. That means I did not care if I did not have the ability before he asked, because his word said, "Red, I need you to do." With that command there came that ability, that endowment, that power, and that might in my inner man.

I am telling you that you do not have to get the word from me. You do not have to get the word from another person. You have heard God's word for your life. Now let the endowment and the power in the inner man rise upon you to endow you with the might and the ability. If you could not do it before He asked, just because He told you, now you can.

Verse 20 in Ephesians 3 says, *Now unto him that is able to do exceeding abundantly above all that we ask or think, according to the power that worketh in us.* The power is going to work *in* us, because that is where the power lies. We are looking for the answer outside versus looking for the answer inside. We wanted somebody to be the answer versus allowing God to be the answer. I bring the thunder, so it does not matter what I encounter. It does not matter how long it takes, because I bring the thunder. Some answers manifest quickly; some things take a long time to come to pass; but you know what? I have patience, and I bring the thunder. It is not if it happens; but when it happens, because it is going to happen. Therefore, it is not over until it happens. It will happen because it is the word of God. Numbers 23:19 says, *God is not a man, that he should lie; neither the son of man, that he should repent: hath he said, and shall he not do it? or hath he spoken, and shall he not make it good?* I am not looking for somebody to make it come to pass, if He spoke it to me. I am not looking for somebody else to change it or allow it to happen if He spoke it to me. That is my word He said. So let it come out of me.

Hopefully, now those of you who have been resisting God will cease from resisting Him. You are going to know that there is more in you than you thought, and it is not just you, it is God Himself. If you generalize God, you will still look at Him as on the throne. You do not see Him in you. Remember that God Himself is also the Spirit of God that lives in you. It is not another spirit that He has and possesses in heaven. It is that same Spirit that He said, "I will come in you and I will live in you. I will be in you and I will be a God." What is too hard for Him to do? There is nothing too hard, because the God is in you.

It is not whether God can do anything or not. The only thing He is going to attach Himself to is the will, because there are three that bear witness, the Spirit, the Son, and the Father. And those three are one. They are not at odds against each other. So whatever the Father wants, the Son is thinking, and whatever the Son is thinking, the Spirit can do. This is why we are going to walk in victorious living. We are going to walk as overcomers. We are going to walk as more than conquerors. We are not going to be running from anything. We are going to be overcomers of everything. We are not maintaining, but we are obtaining. We are not just trying to keep it, but we are trying to take it. See, that is why you cannot keep your mind on you, because when you have your mind on you, you are just trying to make sure your mind do not get lost. I am not worrying about what I am losing, because I am not losing anything. I am gaining. 2 Timothy 1:7 says, *For God hath not given us the spirit of fear*. He is talking about the Spirit. *But of power*. He has given us a spirit of power, spirit of love, and the spirit of a sound mind. Do you see He said He has not given you the spirit of fear, but He *has given* you the power, love, and sound mind? He is giving you His Spirit that empowers you.

The Father's Will Is Results

I want you to know and understand three important facts about the triune parts of God. All Jesus wanted to do is think the Father's will. All that the Spirit of God wants to do is perform the Father's will. The Father's will is that He just wants to love you. Not only does He want to love you, but He also wants to show love through you to others. He said, "Can I allow the ability that is in you to be sent through you and experienced in others?" Romans 15:19 says, *Through mighty signs and wonders, by the power of the Spirit of God; so that from Jerusalem, and round about unto Illyricum, I have fully preached the gospel of Christ.* This is where I want to conclude chapter 6; if you are not getting signs or wonders, it is not by the might of the Spirit of God. The Spirit of God is not a shaking, or even a feeling; the Spirit of God is results. You have no evidence of the Spirit of God in you if you have no evidence of the results of God in you and around you.

The anointing is going to change you on the inside and then it is going to change everything around you. That is the evidence of being endowed by the Spirit of God. If others are not being convinced that He lives then it is because there is no evidence of the Spirit of God in you. Genesis 1:2 says, *The Spirit of God moved upon the face of the waters.* How many of you know that everything that was created was created by the Spirit of God? What we see in creation is the evidence of His signs and wonders. What we see in Genesis was the muscle of God performing the will and word of God.

God said, "Who made it happen?" Where is that Spirit now? Is that Spirit still in heaven? Where is that Spirit? Where does that

Spirit rest and abide? In us, so when God said, "What is going to move on the face of this earth and make it happen?" He means the Spirit of God on us. So why are you waiting on something else to happen when you have the Spirit of God to make it happen. He did not tell anybody else to do it; He told you. He did not reveal it to others; He revealed it to us.

Deuteronomy 6:5 says, *And thou shalt love the Lord thy God with all thine heart, with all thy soul, and with all thy might.* When you love God with all your heart, your mind, your soul, and might then that is the fullness of God's love shown in you. When your heart lines up with God's word, when your mind lines up with God's word, and when your might lines up with God's word, then that is when the love of God is shown in its fullness toward God. You cannot tell me that you love God when you will give Him your heart and your soul, but you will not give Him your might. We understand that Jesus said, "I am the way, I am the truth, and the life," and we learned that you must choose the way, think the truth, and experience the life. God has added on to this revelation with this: the way leads to the Father, the truth tells of the Son, and the life is through the power of the Holy Ghost. So you must choose and walk the way, think and speak the truth, and you have to live and experience the life. In doing these things, you show your love toward the Father.

Again, I am going to say it one more time. Jesus said, "*I am the way, I am the truth, and the life,*" and the way leads to the Father, the truth speaks of the Son, and the life is through and by the Holy Ghost and His power. So now you must choose and walk the way. You have to think and speak the truth, and you have to live and experience the life. When you do all of that, then you will achieve the fullness of all that you are—spirit, soul, and body. This is showing God that you love Him that much.

Those that love God obey His commandments. Remember the rich young ruler, who asked Jesus what must he do to inherit eternal life? Jesus told him the commandments and the young man said, "I obeyed all of these from my youth." Yet Jesus told him he lacked one thing. What was the one thing he lacked? The young man had the ability to hear and to read and to do the law, but when Jesus told him to do a specific thing he would not do it. That young man lacked *instant* obedience. Jesus told him, *Go and sell all that you have and follow me.* That was His word for that moment. If he would have obeyed *that* one, then he would have been all right. That is the test we must pass today. You obey all these words, all these commandments, but the very command you lack is the one He is telling you to do now. Go tell them you love them; go do this; or go do that, and you are still refusing to do it. God said you obeyed all these commandments, but you still lack one. You lack the one I am telling you to do now. Choose and walk the way. Think and speak the truth, and when you do that, you will live and experience the life. This means the end results will be manifestation and the life in abundance that He came to give you. Yet remember, you cannot *do* until you have the anointing of God on your flesh to get the results.

CHAPTER 7

The Final Level

I think God has been preparing the body of Christ for years and years for something special to take place through us. I think that we are the generation, we are the group, and we are the believers that will start believing what God said and allow God to do that which He has always wanted to do. Our growth is essential to God's plan, and we have decided to participate by learning who we are and how our development relates to God.

Thus far, we have discussed all three aspects of this process. We understand that God is a triune God, God the Father, God the Son, and God the Holy Spirit, and how each part of God develops each part of man. We have also learned that in order for our development to be successful, it has to be done in the right order.

We cannot desire the anointing of God that is produced by the Spirit of God on the flesh to come forth to do what we decide. For the anointing by itself will not renew our minds to line up with what God wants. The Spirit of God will not be in conflict, or be at odds or be at war against the rest of God. The fullness of God comes in place and is released by your yielding to have His place as Father. I am not saying that you cannot see bits and pieces of the anointing, but we are talking about maximizing God's potential in you.

In addition, you cannot get the Father's instruction until you get your mind renewed. In this Jesus is the way, Jesus is the path, Jesus is the door, Jesus is the bridge, and Jesus does not speak of Himself. He directs you to the Father so that the Father can speak for Himself.

Therefore, we have concluded that God the Father wants to develop our spirit man, and God the Son develops our mind by renewing the way that we think. You should be convinced by now that the word is to get you established in thinking in line with what God wants. So, when the Father tells you what to do specifically, the Spirit of God can come up on your flesh to help you to live the life that He came to give you.

Now we have reached the climax of *Developing the Complete You* where we talk about achieving the final level. My goal in the phrase *final level*, is to release or to unleash what is already in you. Settle the fact that you have it all. We are trying to get to a level of maturity to where we realize that we do not have to go to God and ask Him for anything else because whatever God is going to do, He has already done. Now we need to go ahead and thank Him and allow it to happen in our lives. Again, the goal is to get to that final level of maturity to where we can release what is already in us.

Philippians 3:14 states, *I press toward the mark for the prize of the high calling of God in Christ Jesus.* When you look at the words *I press*, it implies you are going to experience some opposition; your journey is not going to be a cakewalk. We already touched on the fact that the devil is not going to allow you to tiptoe through the tulips without some kind of resistance. Religion can give the false impression that when you get born again and in the will of God, that is all it takes for you to have a stress-free life. In truth, it can be stress-free, but it is not an obstacle-free life. In this world, you shall have tribulation. Being saved does not keep you from troubles. Being saved gives you the ability to overcome troubles. Nobody is convinced when you are not walking in victory; and you are not walking in victory, when you are avoiding the conflict because avoidance is not victory. As a saved born-again believer, our testimony and our witness is the victory that we live in our lives. This means when people are going through the things we went through; we can tell them how to get out because we got out. If we did not get out of that trouble, we cannot convince them that they cannot get out. How can you convince anybody of what they can do when you cannot do it?

So again, it is not an obstacle-free life that we are looking to live. We should look forward to the battles because the battles will only verify who we are and bring glory to God that we are who we are. We bring the light to the forefront in the midst of the darkness. You do not need to turn on the light when everything is already lit. Light is not effective in the midst of light. For instance, many times we are at our best when we come to church. However, you do not need to be at your best when you come to church because there is not much happening here that will come against you. I am not saying things do not happen in church, but for the most part the trouble that you encounter is when you leave the church. Your church should be a safe haven. It should be a place where you come and get equipped. You should not come to church ready to fight or looking for a fight. You should be looking to get equipped so that when you leave, and the fight comes, you know that you have the power to overcome it.

Again, the scripture states, *I press toward the mark*; the word *mark* is a place. The mark is a destination. We are talking about that final level, and that mark is the level. The mark indicates where the prize is located. You must always look at where you are going because if you do not put emphasis on the prize or the mark, then you are not going to be willing to make the journey. Or you are going to allow what you encounter along the way to deter you from wanting to reach the mark. So where is the emphasis in your life? What you are dealing with, or where you are going to end up? Is where you are going to end up worth the issues that you are dealing with? We need to get to the point that wherever God wants us to be is worth whatever we have to go through to get there. That means there is no surrender and there is no retreat; no backing up, no being passive, and no going around. We are going through, and it starts with preparation.

The word *level* also means height, position, or rank. It is a size in a scale. Let me remind you that God is trying to get us to that final level. When I use the word *final*, I do not mean as in *the* finality, or that there is not another level. What I am saying is that at this moment, there is a final level that you need to reach. Once you obtain that, you will find out that there is another level. Yet do not need to be concerned about the other levels until you get to *this* final level of where you are. For all of us, there is a level in God that we know we should reach and have not reached yet. As we reach different levels, more is exposed, but at the level you are on, there are some things that are exposed that you have not yet dealt with. That is keeping you from getting to the level that you know that you can reach. So we need to get there.

Luke 12:48 states, *But he that knew not, and did commit things worthy of stripes, shall be beaten with few stripes. For unto whomsoever much is given, of him shall be much required: and to whom men have committed much, of him they will ask the more.* This is the thing that I want you to understand; all of us should want more from God. We should be content in the stages that we are, but we should not be complacent in those stages. We should always be striving for better. Again, the sign of God's hands being upon anything is excellence, or increase. This means when God is doing what He is doing in your life, it is increasing. If you are not growing in the things of God, you will begin to increase in the things of the devil, because you cannot stay the same unless you are increasing at a certain rate of level.

Excellence

If you ever had the question of how can I judge if I am getting better, here is the answer God revealed to me. He said, "Do not judge your life on all that you do, because if you look at that, you are going to see more that you could have done, more you should have done. Judge your life if it's getting better. If your tomorrow is better than today, then you are getting better. If your next week is getting better than this week, then you are getting better. You may not even be all that you want to be, but if you are getting better, you will arrive at the place that I want you to be."

Staying at one level will never satisfy you. For example, you can have a million dollars, and if you have a million dollars for a long period of time, that is not going to be enough. If a million dollars is all that you have and there is no way to get more, I promise you that after a while, you are going to be looking for ways to get more money. You realize there are many things you can do with the million dollars, and that if you do not increase any more, that income will eventually run out. You have an expectation to want more and you are propelled to do more to achieve your goal. Whether you understand it or not, that is just the drive of God on you to excel. Realize that God wants to bring increase to your life, but in order to do so, God will require more from your life. *For unto whomsoever much is given, of him shall be much required.*

We do not mind God increasing us; we just do not want Him to require more from us. Have you considered that to reach the place of destiny that God has for you, there is a cost? Are you ready, prepared, and willing to do what is necessary? Many of us know what God wants us to do or know the requirements on our lives, but we do not want the journey to get to the end. The journey is important because it prepares you for the end. Also, you should never do things at all cost to get to the end. There is no point of getting to the final level if you are not prepared and cannot stand at the end.

The journey through to the final level teaches us to handle things as they come and to develop endurance through it. I reiterate a statement that I made in a previous chapter that avoidance is not victory. Do not try to avoid the conflict, because you do not know what you are going to need, or what endurance you are going to have, or what understanding you will have to be in until you go through the steps and process to get to the end.

God is not trying to put you on a roller-coaster ride on your journey to the final level. Pressing toward the mark requires for you to have a specific mentality to help you obtain and withstand to the end. John 14:1-3 says, *Let not your heart be troubled: ye believe in God, believe believe also in me. In my Father's house are many mansions: if it were not so, I would have told you. I go to prepare a place for you. And if I go and prepare a place for you, I will come again, and receive you unto myself; that where I am, there ye may be also.* God starts off by giving us the mind-set that we should possess, *Let not your heart be troubled, believe in me.*

He did not say you were not going to have trouble. He said do not be troubled by the trouble. That is a good way to think and behave because even though trouble comes, it does not mean that trouble should overcome. You can look at it as being an obstacle or opportunity, a stumbling block or a stepping stone. You can look at it as something that is going to make you worse or make you better. You can view it as something that is going to expose a weakness or reveal strength.

Again, let's look at John 14, Jesus said, *Let not your heart be troubled: ye believe in God, believe also in me. In my Father's house are many mansions: if it were not so, I would have told you. I go to prepare a place* (that place is the mark) *for you. And if I go and prepare a place for you, I will come again, and receive you unto myself: that where I am, there ye may be also.* Let us go down to verse 6 where Jesus says, *I am the way, the truth and the life: no man cometh unto the Father, but by me.* We talked about this stage of development where we should choose the way, think the truth, and experience the life. Choosing the way is walking the way, thinking the truth is speaking the truth, and experiencing the life is living the life. That means we must get to the point that our life is a reflection of the life He came to give us. That means we are not just speaking the truth and not just seeing the results; we are speaking the truth and living what we spoke. This is that final place. It is not just a thought or it is not just words; it is actually the life that we are living and we going to get there.

Honesty Is the Best Policy

Another aspect of getting to and achieving the final level also requires us to be honest with ourselves. There is a saying, *To thine own self be true.* Earlier we touched on how God does not need your faith when you come to Him; God needs your truth. God cannot deal with you when you do not acknowledge where you are. God cannot deal with you when you do not acknowledge that there is a weakness. The first step of deliverance is realizing and acknowledging that you need to be delivered. The first step of being made better is realizing that you need to be made better and that you can be made better. Yet if you think that you have already arrived at that place, then you are not going to do anything to get to that other place. I am telling you that you need to allow the truth that is in you to be revealed in the truth of God to be magnified in your life.

Ephesians 4:15 says, *But speaking the truth in love, may grow up into him and all things, which is the head, even Christ.* Speaking the truth in love will help you to grow. Not only will speaking the truth in love help you, but it will also affect your love for one another. See, we are quick to speak the truth to someone else to their face or about someone behind closed doors. However, can you love God enough to speak the truth about yourself so that you can grow up? When you have an issue, can you speak the truth and say, "God, you know what? I need help in this!" When people still get on your nerves, can you speak the truth about it and say, "God, you know what? I need some strength on how to deal with people, because I am not a people person, I do better by myself. Please help me." This is just a side note, but it will help you in obtaining the final level; you are never going to maximize God's potential in your life being by yourself. It will never happen, because everything that

God has is for people. Everything that God is doing in your life is for people. Every gift, calling, and anointing that He is going to equip you with is for people. Remember, we are talking about the final level, and to get to this level, we must have truth.

Being truthful is essential. You need to know where you are on your journey. See, the first rule of travel is to know your starting point when going to your destination. You cannot chart a course from place to place if you do not identify two points, where you are and where you are going. You may know where you are going, but have you identified where you are? Truthfully, some of you are calling yourself something that you are not, and God cannot work with a lie. Religiously, you may be saying, "No, I am speaking faith," but again, He does not need your faith; He needs your truth. You can speak faith to me, but you speak the truth to Him.

Romans 12:1 says, *I beseech you therefore, brethren, by the mercies of God, that ye present your bodies a living sacrifice, holy, acceptable unto God which is your reasonable service. And be not conformed to this world: but be ye transformed by the renewing of your mind, that ye may prove what is that good, and acceptable, and perfect, will of God. For I say, through the grace given unto me, to every man that is among you, not to think of himself more highly than he ought to think; but to think soberly, according as God hath dealt to every man the measure of faith.* You see, in this verse He is talking about the measure of faith, but when it comes to making changes in your life for the better, you still need to think in line with where you are.

It is essential to come to God and speak the truth to Him when it is dealing with your growth because God cannot work with a lie. Did you know that? He cannot increase a lie; He will not increase a lie. God is not looking for a whole lot of anything to multiply. He is looking for the right thing to multiply. In other words, if you bring a lot of lies, if He were to multiply what you brought, there would only be bigger lies. Yet if you bring a seed of a truth, then He can touch that seed of truth and increase it to make it more than what you started out with, but it has to be truth.

We are still focused on getting to that final level, and we are talking about increase; the increase is God releasing something in you that has been sitting idly by and waiting to produce all that He wants to produce. However, truth has a major part to play in what God wants to do in us, for us, and through us. Ephesians 6:12 says, *For we wrestle not against flesh and blood, but against principalities, against powers, against the rulers of the darkness of this world, against spiritual wickedness in high places. Wherefore, take unto you the whole armour of God, that ye may be able to withstand in the evil day, and having done all, to stand. Stand therefore.* Immediately after we are directed to stand, God starts describing the parts of the whole armor of God and explaining to us what to put on. Verse 14 says to *stand therefore, having your loins girt about with truth.* It is not by chance that the first garment He told you to put on was truth, and where did He tell you to place the garment of truth? *To gird* means to circle around your loins. Why there? This is where your reproductive organs are located, and God cannot reproduce anything if it is not based on truth. That is why the devil cannot create anything because he has no truth in him, and that is why God cannot lie, because He is all truth. Unless you put on truth around your increase, He cannot increase your increase. I do not care what kind of truth it is, but He can deal with ugly truth as long as it is open.

Please, make a decision to get rid of the hidden truth in your life. Sometimes people can hide things so well and for so long, that they will not even acknowledge that it exists. That is called deceiving yourself. Therefore, we must operate in truth, no matter what it is. At the end of this book, you are going to have an opportunity to confront the truth in you if you are open, if you are honest, if you are real, and if you really want to go to that next and final level. So let me go over again what the final level is. The final level is developing the complete you and the manifestation of all that God wants and have in your life. It is manifested when the triune God comes together in the triune you and manifests all of God in all of you.

We have seen the Spirit of God, and some of us have yielded to the Spirit of God in some form or fashion. We see the word of God, and some of us are yielded to the word of God in some form or fashion. We have experienced the Father's love, and some of us have yielded and experienced that. The issue is we have not totally and completely in every aspect of our lives yielded to the Father, the Son, and the Holy Ghost in our spirit, soul, and body. Not in all ways and not in all cases. This is why we are having a roller coaster of a ride that we call a life of Christianity. This is why we are not seeing the fullness of God's manifestation in our lives and we are "sometimes up, sometimes down, and sometimes level to the ground." The final level involves increase, and God's hand on anything is increased by his hand. God wants to love you and deliver you from everything that holds you back from giving Him your all. In the last chapter, we will address what God's roles are in this process and what He will require from you.

CHAPTER 8

Fire and Love

If you have made it to this final chapter in *Developing the Complete You*, it is safe to assume you are ready for God to do some extraordinary things in your life. We left off in chapter 7 with the understanding that we have to approach God with the truth about ourselves in order for Him to manifest His will through us. Once we have acknowledged our faults, there is a process that we have to yield ourselves to. This process involves the essence of God coming in contact with our truth and making a lasting change that will affect us and those with whom we interact. In this final portion, we are going to learn the importance of God as love and fire, and how these traits of God help us to access the final level.

The love of God is the essence of the Father, and in the Bible God the Father is always represented as fire. Therefore when we look at *the fire* and *the love* in God's word, they are both synonymous with Father. One of the things we realize and understand when we look at developing the fullness of man is that Jesus did not come to testify and speak of Himself; He only spoke that which the Father told Him to say. So He was not speaking His word, and when you look at that which is written in red, we know that is Jesus speaking, but it is not really Jesus speaking. If we say Jesus is the word, then whose word is He? He is the Father's word. I mention this because we need to believe that the Father is speaking in the Bible to us, and not just Jesus. Again, I thank God for Jesus, but Jesus is the bridge, the door, and the path that only leads us to that place and that place is the intimate and personal relationship with the Father. We have to see the Father's expression in our lives in order to maximize Jesus' effect in our lives. Also, you will never see the anointing until you get your thinking in line with this concept. The anointing is not going to do anything other than what the Father wants.

Now we are going to get down to God the Father who always represented himself in the fire. Think about that fire in the scripture when it refers to how a candle was not lit to be put under a bushel but lit to be put on a candlestick. We have the light of God in us, but where are we putting it? Starting from Hebrews 12:23–25, the word sates, *To the general assembly and church of the firstborn, which are written in heaven, and to God the Judge of all, and to the spirits of just men made perfect, and to Jesus the mediator of the new covenant, and to the blood of sprinkling, that speaketh better things than that of Abel. See that ye refuse not him that speaketh. For if they escaped not who refused him that spake on earth, much more shall not we escape, if we turn away from him that speaketh from heaven.* Here is the thing that you must understand; God is going to shake up the world, all of heaven and earth, only we have not seen this yet. We have not seen it because we have been refusing Him who speaks from heaven. We rejected Him who spoke from the earth, but now He is trying to speak directly to us from heaven. Verse 26–27 reads, *Whose voice then shook the earth: but now he hath promised, saying, Yet once more I shake not the earth only, but also heaven. And this word, Yet once more, signifieth the removing of those things that are shaken, as of things that are made, that those things which cannot be shaken may remain.* That means that there is going to be a shaking in your life, and the only thing that is going to remain is that thing that is of God.

That is a good thing. You should want everything that is not of God to be shaken away. It does not matter how much is left, because if it is all God that is left, that is what He wants to increase. See, we want to hold on to a lie just because it is a lie. We may have a whole lot, but it may not be a whole lot of God. Verse 28–29 reads, *Wherefore we receiving a kingdom which cannot be moved, let us have grace, whereby we may serve God acceptably with reverence and godly fear: For our God is a consuming fire.* Let that same fire be released in you today.

The fire is God's love, but it is a consuming fire. That means when it is released, there are no hidden areas in your life that are safe. When fire touches whatever it touches, it will be known. If you are wood, you are going to be consumed. If you are gold, then you are going to be made better. What makes some pieces of gold more precious than other pieces? The amount of heat that has been put on it is what makes it special. So what is going to make you more precious? We have been containing God's love, this fire, in us and not allowing it to have free rein in our lives to touch all of our lives. We have been having certain doors shut. He can touch this or that, but He cannot touch this. God said, "Unless I touch it, it is not going to be made better. Unless I put my hand on it and consume whatever needs to be consumed or purify whatever needs to be purified, it is only going to be what it is."

God has always represented Himself in fire. In Genesis 15:17, when He cut covenant with Abraham, it was a smoking furnace and a burning lamp that walked between the two halves; this was the Father coming down in his presence. In Exodus 3:1–4, it was Moses on the mountain, and the Father spoke unto him in a flame of fire, out of the midst of a bush. He did not use a substitute. He did it Himself. In 1 Kings 18:30–38, when Elijah was having this contest with the prophets of Baal, it is said the fire of the Lord fell and consumed the burnt sacrifice. Our God is a consuming fire.

Malachi 3:2-3 reads, *But who may abide the day of his coming? and who shall stand when he appeareath? for he is like a refiner's fire and like fuller's soap: And he shall sit as a refiner and purifier of silver: and he shall purify the sons of Levi.* He is talking about touching each and every thing. Did you know that we are the priests of our homes? Unlike in the Old Testament, we do not have to have another form of priesthood to go before us to the throne of God, because He has made all of us kings and priests of our own lives. Just as He touched the Levites, He has to touch your life. This is what I was referring to at the beginning of the chapter when I talked about accessing the final level. When we allow God to touch us in every area of our lives that is when we have true access to God.

Do you remember reading how Moses had to wear a veil to shield his face? It was because the Israelites could not look upon his face directly in their sinful state. Moses had been in the presence of God for so long that the glory was too bright to look upon. The light of God was so blinding, and God's presence will not tolerate sin! Anything can change when it comes to God and His presence, and your sin or your issue is no different. I am not talking issues that you were unaware of in your life because sin is not sin until it is known. If there is not a speed limit on a sign, then speeding is not against the law. The whole issue with Adam and Eve was they did not know good and evil. They only knew of good; but when they had the knowledge of good and evil, they could be judged of evil. They may not have done anything differently after they got the knowledge, but they knew it was wrong to disobey God, and they still did it.

The same principle applies to you. God covers you until you come to the knowledge of what is evil, but once you come to the knowledge, it becomes sin and you know it is wrong and you still do it. Do you think that with that sin present you still have total access to the Father, without being consumed? I know you probably think, "Jesus covers my sin." He has covered your sin, but you cannot abide just in sin alone and think it is all right. He said for you to draw nigh to Him and He will draw nigh to you. How do you draw nigh to Him? You draw near to God by allowing Him to have access to all of you, the good, the bad, and the ugly.

Where you are is not the issue; it is what you refuse to change that becomes the issue. It is also not Him being able to deal with the issue; it is you not allowing Him or wanting Him to deal with it that becomes the issue. You are being comfortable in your sin, satisfied, and that will always stifle His ability to do more than what He is doing. You have to let Him have it. Remember when much is given, much is required. If you really want more, then you have to let Him have more of you. Let His consuming fire touch it.

You know we talk about the three Hebrew boys—Shadrach, Meshach, and Abednego, in Daniel 3:19, but the thing we fail to realize is that in the Old Testament, there was not a separation of the Father, the Son, and the Holy Spirit. You see a lot of mixture of words that signify the either one or the other. It depended upon what was needed at the time. When we look at Daniel 3, it reads, *I see four men loose, walking in the midst of the fire.* We thought Jesus came into the fire with the three men, but the only thing Jesus did was manifest his presence because He was already in the fire. He was already in the fire, because that fire was a representation of God. You do not believe me? Jesus' presence is why those who were binding the Hebrew boys were consumed before they were put in the furnace. Jesus' presence was the reason why Shadrach, Meshach, and Abednego did not even have a smell of smoke on them. What you have to realize about our Father is that Jesus was abiding in the Father's love. When He was needed, He revealed Himself to three Hebrews boys.

See, some of us think that Satan is going to be ruling and reigning in the lake of fire, but how many of you know that the lake of fire is really the sentence to the devil? He is not ruling anything in hell. There has been a misconception of what hell is all about. You think that the devil is going to be ruling and reigning in hell, but no, he is not. God still rules hell. Hell is not the devil's kingdom because he does not have a kingdom. Satan has a sentence for eternity, and he is just trying to get some folks to come down to be a part of his sentence. He is not going to be ruling anything.

How can he be contained in himself? He is going back to where he came from. The devil came out of God, and he is going back to that same place. Psalms 139:7–8 says, *Whither shall I go from thy spirit? or whither shall I flee from thy presence? If I ascend up into heaven, thou art there: if I make my bed in hell, behold, thou art there.* Do you see that? That means God is still ruling above and beneath. You have to believe that consuming fire will be in hell, and do you want to know what is going to be the torment? People are going to have the opportunity to experience God's love without having the opportunity to walk in it. They are going to see all the things that could have happened in their lives if they would have given their lives to God and now they are not going to have an opportunity to experience it, and they are going to be tormented. It is going to be like the guy who is extremely thirsty and is so close to a glass of ice cold water, but he is not able to touch it; to be this close to a hug and not be able to receive it. They are going to be in the midst of all of this goodness and cannot feel it. You have all this wisdom, knowledge, and understanding and cannot use it, because you did not make the right decision when you had the opportunity. That is going to be the torment; the love of God and the fire of God.

Again the fire and the love are the same thing. In John 1, the Bible talks about how God is love. If our God is a consuming fire and our God is love, the love is the fire. God has to touch our lives with love and fire. We need Him to purify us so we can love others as He loves us. Acts 2:1-4 reads, *And when the day of Pentecost was fully come, they were all with one accord in one place. And suddenly there came a sound from heaven as of a rushing mighty wind, and it filled all the house where they were sitting. And there appeared unto them cloven tongues like as of fire, and it sat upon each of them. And they were all filled with the Holy Ghost, and began to speak with other tongues, as the Spirit gave them utterance.* From these verses we can clearly see how the unity and oneness is necessary for the fullness of God to take place or manifest. You cannot be unified and one with anyone until you are unified and one with yourself. If your mind and your body are at odds or in conflict with each other, then that is going to be a hindrance from you being able to connect with the rest of the brothers and sisters in the church.

I have made the following statements of why I believe the body of Christ cannot come together; it is because the body in the local church cannot come together. When you sit in the seat next to one another and cannot come together with one another, you do not have that which is necessary to come together with the other churches that are part of the body of Christ. Because insecurity will breed insecurity, fear will always breed fear. The next reason you cannot come together with the people next to you is because you cannot come together in your own household. There are some issues with your biological brother and sisters, and there are some issues with people that came out of the same lineage with you. Until you get those things settled, there are going to be some hindrances in your life. You cannot love somebody whom you just met, and not love the one that came out of the same parent. Do you see what I am saying? There is going to be a hindrance. Finally, I know why you cannot love your brothers and your sisters or wife or children. Do you want to know why you cannot love them? It is because you cannot love yourself.

We need to remedy this situation by embracing God's fire and love. I am telling you something that is life changing, because when you have a love in you that came from God, then that love in you will always affect the loving around you. Love extends itself beyond itself. Those that have a good relationship with themselves have good relationships with their family members. Those that have good relationships with their family members have good relationships with people in the church. Those that have good relationships with people in the church have good relationships with people who are a part of other churches.

Now consider all that I said, and if you have a problem with it, then you need to find where your issue is, and that is where your problem is. For instance, if you have a problem with people in the church, it is because you have a problem at home. If you got a problem at home, it is because you got a problem in you. The love of God is an all-consuming fire. The love of God is a never-ending, never-failing fire. The love of God is a fire that will consume all and cannot be denied by any. Love never fails.

Let us look at John 13:34–35, which says, *A new commandment I give unto you, That ye love one another; as I have loved you, that ye also love one another. By this shall all men know that ye are my disciples, if ye have love one to another.* We take this as Jesus talking to his disciples. No, this is the Father talking to His children. This is God talking to us. Jesus did not speak His own words; Jesus spoke the words of the Father. He was in total submission, so this can apply to us even if Jesus was talking to those twelve or those thirty-two or those one hundred or whatever the number of people was who were around Him. We still can say we are His disciples if we have love for one another. We are His disciplined ones, we are His children, and we are the ones who are called by His name if we love one another. Love, God's love, is how those in the world are going to know or identify us. That is the DNA test that we have that we can give that signifies what family we belong to; we can tell if His love is flowing.

Mathew 24:4–5 states, *And Jesus answered and said unto them, Take heed that no man deceive you. For many shall come in my name, saying, I am Christ; and shall deceive many.* There are certain leaders of churches that can be extremely intrusive and domineering with their members, but one of the things that I am bound and determined to do is that I will not be God for anyone. I do not want to be God, but I am trying to direct you to God. I want to be able to direct you to hear the Father for yourself. I want to be able help you understand Jesus and renew your mind through the word for yourself. I want to be able to help you know how to release and yield to the Spirit of God in you so that the power of God can be magnified in all that you do for yourself. I am not trying to be your power, not trying to be your thought, not trying to be His voice, but I am trying to get you to develop this relationship for yourself. See, you cannot be deceived when you develop your own personal relationship, because everything will either be a confirmation or a denial. When you know for yourself that you are hearing God, you are not so apt to be deceived to do what someone else says that God said. However, when you do not know him for yourself, it is time to grow up to get to know Him. You will never grow up in a relationship with God by hiding things, because a child hides things. A grown-up will take responsibility for his actions and know that they will have to face the consequences.

Matthew 24:5–12 says, *For many shall come in my name, saying, I am Christ; and shall deceive many. And ye shall hear of wars and rumours of wars: see that ye be not troubled: for all these things must come to pass, but the end is not yet. For nation shall rise against nation, and kingdom against kingdom: and there shall be famines, and pestilences, and earthquakes, in divers places. All these are the beginning of sorrows. Then shall they deliver you up to be afflicted, and shall kill you: and ye shall be hated of all nations for my name's sake. And then shall many be offended, and shall betray one another, and shall hate one another. And many false prophets shall rise, and shall deceive many. And because iniquity shall abound, the love of many shall wax cold.* What is the reason for the cold? When there is no love, things get cold. But when there is love, there is warmth, and there is heat. There is a fire that drives you to do and motivates you in spite of everything else. 1 John 2:4–6, it says, *He that saith, I know him, and keepeth not his commandments, is a liar, and the truth is not in him. But whoso keepeth his word, in him verily is the love of God perfected: hereby know we that we are in him. He that saith he abideth in him ought himself also so to walk, even as he walked.* And how did He walk? He walked in love. God so loved the world that He gave, and believe that every act that Jesus performed was an act of love from the Father. It was love, or another term is compassion, that motivated Jesus and allowed Him to endure the cross. It was that love. What causes you to go through the things you go through? If it is not motivated by love, then you do not have the strength or the power or the juice to produce.

1 John 3:1–2 says, *Behold, what manner of love that the Father has bestowed upon us, that we should be called the sons of God: therefore the world knoweth us not because it knew him not. Beloved, now we are the sons of God, and it doth not yet appear what we shall be: but we know that, when he shall appear, we shall be like him; for*

we shall see him as he is. He said all things that are hidden shall now be revealed. If I know that He is love, then I know what I should look like. If I know that this is His motivation, then I should know what I should act like. And verse 16–18 says, *Hereby perceive we the love of God, because he laid down his life for us: and we ought to lay down our lives for the brethren. But whoso hath this world's good and seeth his brother have need, and shutteth up his bowels of compassion from him, how dwelleth the love of God in him? My little children, let us not love in word, neither in tongue; but in deed and in truth.* Verse 23–24 says, *And this is his commandment, That we should believe on the name of his Son Jesus Christ, and love one another, as he gave us commandment. And he that keepeth his commandments dwelleth in him, and he in him. And hereby we know that he abideth in us, by the Spirit which he hath given us.* What are you producing in your life? If it does not resemble the love of God, then you need to rethink some things. What is the sense of deliverance when you are not delivering folks in love or to love? What is the sense of anything being done that you say is God when the motivation was not God's love?

Calling ALL Ministers

If you are reading this book, then God has called you to do something that will benefit others and increase His kingdom. That makes you a minister. So just what is the responsibility of a minister? Hebrews 1:7 reads, *And of the angels he saith, Who maketh his angels spirits, and his ministers a flame of fire.* See, a minister is only a servant of God. We look at that title "minister" and think it is someone who others should cater to. You may think it is a great and awesome title, and it is. However, how are you defining greatness? The Bible says, *Let the greatest among you be the servant of all.* You see, when you classify yourself as a minister, it means you are the greatest servant that God has and God is using you as a fire and a love spreader. This means God's love can be exemplified in all that you do or identified in all that you do. God's love is so evident in what is manifested that it is undeniable, unmistakable, and it has to be God. That is how people are going to be convinced. That is how people are going to be changed; not by much preaching, but by your many works and acts of love. Again, love never fails.

What is the deal with fire and love? Why are they so important? I understand that we have acknowledged and confessed water is of God, water is used of God, and water is used as an expression of the baptism of the Holy Spirit. We signify and identify with water, but water is not the best identifier of the Spirit. In Matthew 3:11, John the Baptist said, *I indeed baptize you with water unto repentance. But he that cometh after me is mightier than I, whose shoes I am not worthy to bear: he shall baptize you with the Holy Ghost, and with fire.*

In my pastorship, I have used water to illustrate certain principles. Like this one: "God, I stand under this fountain as an empty cup, fill me until I overflow," and that is fine. However, one thing that happens with water is that it can run out. Think about this, if I am water and I fill up with water, then I can pour into the next person the water that I have, but as I pour into him, I am being emptied out myself, right? Some of you think that there is nothing wrong with that, because if you are empty you can be filled back up. That is fine; yet remember, we are talking about accessing the final level. When you get to this final level, you will be fire. The thing about fire is, fire can touch something else, get it going, and yet not lose any intensity in itself. Fire is never tired, it is never insufficient, and it is never lacking. I have started something, but yet I am still the same as I was before I started to produce something in another.

The thing about fire is that you cannot make me worse by what you do. I can start you and still not be affected by you because I am self-sufficient in His sufficiency. Consequently, when you come together with me, it will make me better because you cannot make me worse. Adding fire to fire makes more fire, but if someone takes his flame, his leaving does not affect my flame. See, the love is the fire. The love is an unconditional love, which means I can love you even though you do not love me. I can love you and affect you and you not loving me will not affect me, because you can make me better, but you cannot make me worse. We have been trying to be water, and God has been trying to make us fire, and now the fire is going to burn in you.

Fire does not care what it burns; fire just looks to burn. You cannot open up the can of fire and try to put it out. Our God is an all-consuming fire, and when you open up the fire, it is going to burn until it burns everything up. How many of you know that the oil of the anointing is the fuel that the fire needs to burn? The oil of the anointing only comes when you are unified. As I stated previously, being unified is when the will of God and the word of God come together in you with the purpose of God. That is when the oil of anointing is given to you so that you can be equipped to do God's will. And this is the thing, you cannot get the oil doing what you want to do. You can only get the oil when you do what He tells you to do, and when the oil comes, the oil will keep the fire burning.

Fire is a great and useful tool, but you have to understand its purpose and know how to maintain it so it will not get out of control. What you do not want to happen is to be burned up because you misused your resource. When you are not allowing the oil of the anointing to be on your life for its designed purpose, it starts consuming things that it was not meant to consume. It starts consuming your flesh, your finances, and your relationships because it has nothing else to burn, but when your purpose is being felt and being acknowledged and lived out, the oil will start pouring and it will be fuel to the fire to keep burning.

You cannot start it, stop it, or keep it under a bushel until you are ready. You will never get to another level and the place that God wants you to be by keeping it under a bushel. But if you are ready, God wants to touch everything in your life, and there is no safe zone. When He starts burning, everything is going to be consumed, and if it is wood or clay, it will be moved out of your life. But if it is silver or gold, whatever it is, it will be made better and precious. You have to make the decision.

I do not know where you are in your life, but God does, and you are going to have to open up your heart. There are some rooms, there are some doors, and there are some places that He has not had access to. There are some things that He wants to put His hand on and touch it with His love. You do not need to be afraid if He touches it, because if it does not need to be there, you want Him to remove it. If it is what He wants, He will make it better. He loves you like that. Know that He said that He will be the God on the inside of you. There is a Spirit of Him that is living in you that is all sufficiency. He is greater than any situation, any circumstances, and the problem is that you have not released Him to be what He wants to be in you. You have not released Him to do what He can do for you.

The Moment of Truth

Now this is the time for you to make that decision. You did not read this book by accident. This is not about what somebody else is going to do. This is not about what anybody else needs to do. This is between you and God. God is preparing us to get to a level that He wants us to get to, and now, it is time for you to make that decision. I cannot make this choice for somebody else, but I can make this choice for me. I understand where you are because I have been in this place of decision. There have been issues in my life that I have been trying to work on myself. There are some things in my life that I have been doing for myself. I have done what I am encouraging you to do, and that is to turn it all over to God and let God be God. Join me as well as many others who have released the fullness of God in our lives. Pray about this, meditate on this, and if you need to read this book again until you can make a quality decision, please do that. Allow God to minister to you, and once you yield to the final level, there is going to be a sign of acceptance to this. Before He can deal with whatever is wrong, truth has to meet truth. That means you have to acknowledge that there is an issue. Acknowledge that there is a problem. Admit that you need help and that He is your help. Before He can deliver you, you need to know that you need to be delivered. Before He can make you free, you need to know that you are bound up. Before He can be what He needs to be, you need to know that He is able.

Are you willing to pay the price? It will cost you your life, but the life that He has come to give you is more than you can ever give yourself. So if you are ready, allow Him to come, and as He ministers to you, let your spirit, soul, and body be in total surrender. Do not predetermine what you will do, but let Him deal with you. He is going to show you exactly what is going to happen in your life. He is going to show you all those things that have been in darkness that have now come to this light of God. I am telling you that there is going to be a fire that is going to be released in you; there is warmth that is going to be found in you, and it is going to start from the top of your head and go all the way down to the toes. You are going to know without a shadow of doubt that the fullness of God has touched you. You are the ground that is holy. Just let Him deal with you. Let Him show you. Let truth meet truth. Let those things that were covered up be uncovered. Let those things that you have been hiding from God be revealed. It is going to be a release of the fullness of God in your life, and unleashing of the total power of God through your life. Old things will be passed away, and behold, all things will become new. There will be a newness of life, a new determination, and a new motivation.

As I close, I desire that you open up your heart and worship the Lord. The word *worship* means to show a reverence for, an intense devotion, to esteem, to love, and to admire. When you worship Him, you open up your heart totally to the love of God in your life. You give Him access to all of you. Believe in the power of God's Sprit overcoming and overtaking you. It is not the power of me, but God's power being released because of your agreement with Him. As you release your faith, I agree with you with my faith that God in you will be unleashed in you.

Thank you for allowing God in me to minister to you. I believe and know from personal experience that God's fire will consume you—every part of your life, every issue in your life, every infirmity in your life, every lack in your life, and it will bring that abundant life.

Made in the USA
Coppell, TX
24 January 2023

11636169R00090